The Gnostic Gospels of Philip, Mary Magdalene, and Thomas

Inside the Da Vinci Code and Holy Blood, Holy Grail

By Joseph Lumpkin

Joseph B. Lumpkin

The Gnostic Gospels of Philip, Mary Magdalene, and Thomas:
Inside The Da Vinci Code and Holy Blood, Holy Grail

Fifth Estate, Post Office Box 116,
Blountsville, AL 35031.

First Edition

Printed on acid-free paper

Library of Congress Control No: 2006924544

ISBN: 1933580135

Fifth Estate, 2006

Joseph B. Lumpkin

The Gnostic Gospels Of Philip, Mary, and Thomas
Inside The Da Vinci Code and Holy Blood, Holy Grail

Joseph B. Lumpkin

What is Gnosticism?

For centuries the definition of Gnosticism has, in itself, been a point of confusion and contention within the religious community. This is due, in part, to the ever-broadening application of the term. The modern definition of Gnosticism has no relevance to this work, or to any pre-Nicene Gnostic document, for that matter. The theology in place at the time of the writing of the ancient texts being examined should be considered and understood before attempting to render or read a translation. To do otherwise would make cloudy and obtuse the translation.

It becomes the duty of both translator and reader to understand what ideas were being espoused and the terms used to convey those ideas. Having a firm grasp of theology, cosmology, and terms will lead to a clear transmission of the meaning of the text in question.

With this in mind Gnosticism in the first through third centuries A.D. will be discussed in the following pages, which precede the translated text.

The cosmology of Gnosticism is complex and very different from orthodox Christianity. In many ways Gnosticism may appear to be polytheistic. The word Gnostic is based on the word "Gnosis," which means "knowledge." The knowledge of the transcendent God and man's ability to transcend this material world with its lesser gods is how Gnosticism got its name.

To understand some of the basic beliefs of Gnosticism, let us start with common ground between it and modern Christianity. Both believe the world is imperfect, corrupt, and brutal. The blame for this, according to mainstream Christianity, is placed squarely on the shoulders of man himself. With the fall of man, the world was forever changed to the undesirable and harmful place in which we live today. However, Gnostics reject this view as an incorrect interpretation of the creation myth.

According to Gnostics, the blame is not in ourselves, but in our creator. The creator of this world was himself somewhat less than perfect and in fact, deeply flawed, making mankind the children of a lesser god.

In the beginning a supreme being called The Father, The Divine All, The Origin, or The Fullness, emanated the element of existence, both visible and invisible. His intent was not to create but, as light emanates from a flame, so did creation shine forth from God. This manifested the primal element needed for creation. Part of this ethereal material gave form to beings called Aeons. One of these Aeons was called Sophia (Wisdom).

Seeing the Divine flame, Sophia sought to know its origin. She sought to know the very nature of God. Sophia's passion ended in tragedy when she managed to capture a divine and creative spark, which she attempted to duplicate with her own creativity. It was this act that produced beings born outside the higher divine realm.

She cast it away from her, outside that place [the Pleroma], that no one of the immortal ones [the other Aeons] might see it, for she had created it in ignorance..."
[The Nag Hammadi Library, James M. Robinson, Ed, pp.104 (Harper & Row, 1981, San Franscisco)]

The overall realm containing the Fullness of the godhead and Sophia is called the Pleroma or realm of Fullness. The lesser gods created in Sophia's (Wisdom) failed attempt were cast outside the Pleroma and away from the presence of God.

The beings she created were imperfect and oblivious to the supreme God. Her creation contained deities even less perfect than herself. They are called "the powers" or "the rulers." It was one of these flawed, imperfect, spiritually blind beings that became the creator of the material world.

This lesser god contained only part of the original creative spark of the supreme being. He also was created with an imperfect nature caused by his distance in lineage and in spirit from the Divine All or Higher God. Because of his imperfections, the lesser god is called the "Half-Maker."

The creator god, the Half-Maker, and his helpers, the "rulers" or "powers," took the stuff of existence produced by the supreme God and fashioned it into this material world.

Since the rulers have no memory of how they came to be alive, they do not realize they are not true creators. They believe they somehow came to create the material world by themselves. God allows them to remain deceived.

The rulers and the creator god intended to create the material world perfect and eternal, but they did not have it in themselves to do this. What comes forth from a being cannot be greater than the highest part of him, so the world was created flawed and transitory.

Man was created with a dual nature. It is the product of the material world of the rulers with their imperfect essence, and the spark of God that emanated from the Divine All through Sophia, which remained in the creator that persisted to form man. The creator or lesser deity seeks to keep man ignorant of his defective state by keeping him enslaved to this material world and to the lesser gods. By doing so he can continue to receive man's worship and servitude. He does not wish man to recognize or gain knowledge of the true supreme

God. Since he does not know or acknowledge the Father God, he views any attempt to worship anything else as spiritual treason.

Only through the realization of man's true state or through death can he escape. This means the idea of salvation does not deal with original sin or blood payment. Instead, it focuses on the idea of awakening to the fullness of the truth.

Gnostics, in the age of the early church, would preach to converts (novices) about this awakening, saying the novice must awaken the god within himself and see the trap that is the material world. Salvation comes from the recognition or knowledge contained in this spiritual awakening.

Not all people are ready or willing to accept the Gnosis. Many are bound to the material world and are satisfied to be only as and where they are. These have mistaken the creator god for the supreme God and do not know there is anything beyond. These people know only the lower or earthly wisdom and not the higher Wisdom or Sophia above the creator god. They are referred to as "dead."

Since the time of Sophia's mistaken creation, there was an imbalance in the cosmos. God re-established the balance by producing Christ and the Holy Spirit. One being a masculine energy, and the other being a feminine energy. This left only Sophia, now in a fallen and bound state to upset the cosmic equation. To counter this, God produced the man Jesus, who was the perfect fruits of the Pleroma, or stuff of existence which made up the material world.

For those who seek that which is beyond the material world and its flawed creator, the supreme God has sent Messengers of Light to awaken the divine spark of the supreme God within us. This part of us will call to the True God as deep calls to deep. The greatest and most perfect Messenger of Light was the Christ. He is also referred to as The Good, Christ, Messiah, and The Word. He came to reveal the Divine Light to us.

He came to show us our own divine spark and to awaken us to the illusion of the material world and its flawed maker. He came to show us the way back to the divine Fullness. The path to enlightenment is the knowledge sleeping within each of us. Christ came to show us the Christ living in each of us. Individual ignorance or the refusal to awaken our internal divine spark is the only original sin. Christ is the only Word spoken by God that can awaken us. Christ is also the embodiment of the Word itself. He is part of the original transmission from the supreme God that has taken form on the earth to awaken the soul of man so that man may search beyond the material world. The transmission or emanation containing the formless will of God is the Holy Spirit. The Holy Spirit is considered to be a feminine force.

Gnostic texts often use sex as a metaphor for spiritual union and release. Since the Godhead itself has both masculine elements of the Father and Son, and a feminine element of the Holy Spirit, sexual terms are used freely. The sexual metaphor is expanded in the story of the original or Full God giving rise to Sophia (Wisdom) as he spewed forth the essence of everything. Sophia became the creator or mother of both angels and lesser gods, including the creator of the material world.

Sexual duality found in Gnosticism allows for more reverence and acceptance of women in the Gnostic worship. Owing to this, the concept that Mary Magdalene was somehow special to Jesus, as is reported in the <u>Gospel of Philip</u>, or that he may have shared spiritual concepts with her that were unknown to the male apostles, as is told in the <u>Gospel of Mary Magdalene</u>, is not so difficult to comprehend.

To continue the flow of metaphors relating to sex and marriage, images of the Bridal-Chamber are replete throughout the Gospel of Philip. This is alludes to a spiritual place where the union of the Bridegroom who is the Son and the seeking heart of man meet and unite. There is also a secondary meaning of unity where the dual nature of man unites when the Light of spiritual awakening conquers the fleshly or material nature and man is made whole by the Truth.

The sexual metaphors used in the Gnostic texts have fanned the flames of great controversy and speculation. It has been widely accepted that societal norms of the time dictated that Jewish men were to be married by the age of thirty. This certainly applied to Rabbis, since marriage and procreation were considered divine commands. Since Jesus is referred to by the title of Rabbi in the Bible it has been noted that his marital status would have placed him into a very small minority in the culture at the time.

Proceeding from the two points of sexual metaphor in Gnostic literature and the likelihood of marriage among the population of Jewish men, controversy arose when speculation began as to whether Jesus could have married. The flames of argument roared into inferno proportions when the translation of the books of Philip and Mary Magdalene were published.

And the companion (Consort) was Mary of Magdala (Mary Magdalene). The Lord loved Mary more than all the other disciples and he kissed her often on her mouth (the text is missing here and the word "mouth" is assumed). The others saw his love for Mary and asked him: "Why do you love her more than all of us?" The Savior replied, "Why do I not love you in the same way I love her?"   *Gospel of Philip*

Peter said to Mary; "Sister we know that the Savior loved you more than all other women. Tell us the words of the Savior that you remember and know, but we have not heard and do not know. Mary answered him and said; "I will tell you what He hid from you."
The Gospel of Mary Magdalene

Seizing on the texts above, writers of both fiction and non-fiction allowed their pens to run freely amidst conjecture and postulation of marriage and children between Jesus and Mary Magdalene.

The writers of <u>The Da Vinci Code</u> and <u>Holy Blood, Holy Grail</u> took these passages and expanded them into storylines that have held readers captive with anticipation.

Did Jesus take Mary to be his wife? Could the couple have produced children? Gnostic theology leaves open the possibility. Since there is a distinction between the man Jesus and the Light of Christ that came to reside within him, it is not contrary to Gnostic beliefs that Mary was the consort and wife of Jesus. Neither would it be blasphemous for them to have children.

Since nothing can come from the material world that is not flawed, Gnostics do not believe that Christ could have been a corporeal being. Thus, there must be some separation or distinction between Jesus, as a man, and Christ, as a spiritual being born from the supreme, unrevealed, and eternal spirit.

To look closer at this theology, we turn to Valentinus, the driving force of early Gnosticism, for an explanation. Valentinus divides Jesus Christ into two very distinct parts; Jesus, the man, and Christ, the anointed spiritual messenger of God. These two forces met in the moment of Baptism when the Holy Spirit of God came to rest on Jesus and the Christ power entered the body of the perfect creation.

Jesus, the man, became a vessel to the Light of God, called Christ or Messiah. In the Gnostic view we all could and should become Christs, carrying the Truth and Light of God. We are all potential vehicles of the same Holy Spirit that Jesus held within him when he was awakened to the Truth.

This means that the suffering and death of Jesus takes on much less importance in the Gnostic view, since Jesus, although a perfect creation, was simply part of the corrupt world and was suffering the indignities of this world as any man would. In this viewpoint, he could have been married and been a father without disturbing Gnostic theology in the least.

The resurrection of Jesus is viewed as a metaphor and not a physical re-animation. One might say that the resurrection happens to us all when our inner light stands up.

In repeated metaphors throughout Gnostic texts, the grace given by the "Messenger of Light" that allows the Word to be received is called the "Oil of Anointing." The knowledge that awakens the soul of man and allows him to search beyond the material world is contained in "The Word." The knowledge that sets man free from the illusion of the material world and reunites him with the Higher or Supreme God is "The Light."

The Gnostic texts seem to divide man into parts. Although at times it is somewhat unclear, the divisions alluded to may include the soul, which is the will or mind of man; the spirit, which is depicted as wind or air (pneuma) and contains the holy spark, which is the spirit of God in man; and the material human form.

Without the oil or light, the spirit is held captive by the lesser gods, which enslave man. This entrapment is called "sickness." It is this sickness that the Light came to heal and thus set us free. The third part of man, which is his material form, is considered a weight, an anchor, and a hindrance, keeping man attached to the corrupted earthly realm.

Let us read these texts and do as the ancient Gnostics commanded. Wake up! Heal yourself! Seek the Christ within you! Let the oil flow down! Let the Word be heard! Let the Light show you the Truth! Become the Christ you are! Give birth to what is inside you! Let the sleeper awaken!

The History of The Gospel of Philip

The Gospel of Philip is assumed to be one of the sources of Dan Brown's novel, <u>The Da Vinci Code,</u> about Mary Magdalene, Jesus, and their children. The Gospel is one of Gnostic texts found at Nag Hammadi in Egypt in 1945 and belongs to the same collection of Gnostic documents as the more famous Gospel of Thomas.

It has been suggested that the *Gospel of Philip* was written in the second century B.C. If so, it may be one of the earliest documents containing themes that would later be used in apocryphal literature.

A single manuscript of the *Gospel of Philip*, written in Coptic, was found in the Nag Hammadi library. The collection was a library of thirteen papyrus texts discovered near the town of Nag Hammadi in 1945 by a peasant boy. The writings in these codices comprised 52 documents, most of which are Gnostic in nature.

The codices were probably hidden by monks from the nearby monastery of St. Pachomius when the official Christian Church banned all Gnostic literature around the year 390 A.D

It is believed the original texts were written in Greek during the first or second centuries A.D. The copies contained in the discovered clay jar were written in Coptic in the third or fourth centuries A.D.

The *Gospel Of Philip* is a list of sayings focusing on man's redemption and salvation as framed by Gnostic theology.

The *Gospel of Philip* presented here is based on a comparative study of translations from the Nag Hammadi Codex by Wesley W. Isenberg, Willis Barnstone, The Ecumenical Coptic Project, Bart Ehrman, Marvin Meyer, David Cartlidge, David Dungan, and other sources.

Each verse was weighed against the theological and philosophical beliefs held by the Gnostic community at the time in which the document was penned. All attempts were made to render the most accurate meaning based on the available translations and information.

Exact wording was secondary to the conveyance of the overall meaning as understood by the contemporary reader.

When the wording of a verse held two possible meanings or needed expanded definitions, optional translations were placed in parentheses.

The Gospel of Philip

1. A Hebrew makes a Hebrew convert, and they call him a proselyte (novice). A novice does not make another novice. Some are just as they are, and they make others like themselves to receive. It is enough for them that they simply are as they are.

2. The slave seeks only to be set free. He does not hope to attain the estate of his master. The son acts as a son (heir), but the father gives the inheritance to him.

3. Those who inherit the dead are dead, and they inherit the dead. Those who inherit the living are alive. They inherit both the living and the dead. The dead cannot inherit anything. How can the dead inherit anything? When the dead inherits the living one, he shall not die but the dead shall live instead.

4. The Gentile (unbeliever) who does not believe does not die, because he has never been alive, so he could not die. He who has trusted the Truth has found life and is in danger of dying, because he is now alive.

5. Since the day that the Christ came, the cosmos was created, the cities are built (adorned), and the dead carried out.

6. In the days when we were Hebrews we were made orphans, having only our Mother. Yet when we believed in the Messiah (became the ones of Christ), the Mother and Father both came to us.

7. Those who sow in the winter reap in the summer. The winter is this world system. The summer is the other age or dispensation (to come). Let us sow in the world (cosmos) so that we will reap in the summer. Because of this, it is right for us not to pray in the winter. What comes from (follows) the winter is the summer. If anyone reaps in the winter he will not harvest but rather pull it up by the roots and will not produce fruit. Not only does it not produce in winter, but on the Sabbath his field shall be bare.

8. The Christ has come to fully ransom some, to save (restore and heal) others, and to be the propitiation for others. Those who were estranged he ransomed. He purchases them for himself. He saves, heals, and restores those who come to him. These he desires to pledge (in marriage). When he became

manifest he ordained the soul as he desired (set aside his own life), but even before this, in the time of the world's beginning, he had ordained the soul (he had laid down his own life). At his appointed time he came to bring the soul he pledged himself to back to himself. It had come to be under the control of robbers and they took it captive. Yet he saved it, and he paid the price for both the good and the evil of the world.

9. Light and dark, life and death, right and left are brothers. It is impossible for one to be separated from the other. They are neither good, nor evil. A life is not alive without death. Death is not death if one were not alive. Therefore each individual shall be returned to his origin, as he was from the beginning. Those who go beyond the world will live forever and are in the eternal present.

10. The names that are given to worldly things cause great confusion. They contort our perception from the real to the unreal. He who hears "God" does not think of the real, but rather has false, preconceived ideas. It is the same with "Father," "Son," "Holy Spirit," "Life," "Light," "Resurrection," and "Church (the called out ones)," and all other words. They do not recall the real, but rather they call to mind preconceived, false ideas. They learned the reality of human death. They who

are in the world system made them think of the false idea. If they had been in eternity, they would not have designated anything as evil, nor would they have placed things within worldly events (time and place). They are destined for eternity.

11. The only name they should never speak into the world is the name the Father gave himself through the Son. This is the Father's name. It exists that he may be exalted over all things. The Son could not become the Father, unless he was given the Father's name. This name exists so that they may have it in their thoughts. They should never speak it. Those who do not have it cannot even think it. But the truth created names in the world for our sake. It would not be possible to learn the truth without names.

12. The Truth alone is the truth. It is a single thing and a multitude of things. The truth teaches us love alone through many and varied paths.

13. Those who ruled (lower gods) desired to deceive man because they knew man was related to the truly good ones. They took the designation of good and they gave it to those who were not good. They did this so that by way of words they might deceive man and bind him to those who are not good.

When they receive favor, they are taken from those who are not good and placed among the good. These are they who had recognized themselves. The rulers (lower gods) had desired to take the free person, and enslave him to themselves forever. Rulers of power fight against man. The rulers do not want him to be saved (recognize himself), so that men will become their masters. For if man is saved there will be no need for sacrifice.

14. When sacrifice began, animals were offered up to the ruling powers. They were offered up to them while the sacrificial animals were still alive. But as they offered them up they were killed. But the Christ was offered up dead to God (the High God), and yet he lived.

15. Before the Christ came, there had been no bread in the world. In paradise, the place where Adam was, there had been many plants as food for wild animals, but paradise had no wheat for man to eat. Man had to be nourished like animals. But the Christ, the perfect man, was sent. He brought the bread of heaven, so that man could eat as he should.

16. The rulers (lower gods) thought what they did was by their own will and power, but the Holy Spirit worked through them without their knowledge to do her will.

17. The truth, which exists from the beginning, is sown everywhere, and everyone sees it being sown, but only a few see the harvest.

18. Some say that Mary conceived by the Holy Spirit. They are in error. They do not know what they are saying. How can a female impregnate another female? Mary is the virgin whom no power defiled. She is a great problem and curse among the Hebrew Apostles and those in charge. The ruler (lower god) who attempts to defile this virgin, is himself defiled. The Lord was not going to say, "my father in heaven", unless he really had another father. He would simply have said, "my father".

19. The Lord says to the Disciples, "Come into the house of the Father, but do not bring anything in or take anything out from the father's house."

20. Jesus (Yeshua) is the secret name; Christ (messiah) is the revealed name. The name "Jesus" (Yeshua) does not occur in any other language. His name is called "Jesus" (Yeshua). In Aramaic his name is Messiah, but in Greek it is Christ (Cristos). In every language he is called the anointed one. The fact that he

is Savior (Yeshua) could be fully comprehended only by himself, since it is the Nazarene who reveals the secret things.

21. Christ has within himself all things; man, angel, mystery (sacraments), and the father.

22. Those who say that the Lord first died and then arose are in error. He would have to first arise before he could die. If he is not first resurrected, he would die, but God lives and cannot die.

23. No one will hide something highly valuable in something ostentatious (that would draw attention). More often, one places something of great worth within a number of containers worth nothing. This is how it is with the (human) soul. It is a precious thing placed within a lowly body.

24. Some are fearful that they will arise (from the dead) naked. Therefore they desire to rise in the flesh. They do not understand that those who choose to wear the flesh are naked. Those who choose to strip themselves of the flesh are the ones who are not naked.

25. Flesh and blood will not be able to inherit the kingdom of God. What is this that will not inherit? It is that which is upon each of us (our flesh). But what will inherit the kingdom is that which belongs to Jesus and is of his flesh and blood. Therefore he says: "He who does not eat my flesh and drink my blood, has no life in him." What is his flesh? It is the Word, and his blood is the Holy Spirit. He who has received these has food and drink and clothing.

26. I disagree with those who say the flesh will not arise. They are in error. Tell me what will rise so that we may honor you. You say it is the spirit in the flesh and the light contained in the flesh. But you say there is nothing outside of the flesh (material world). It is necessary to arise in this flesh if everything exists within the flesh.

27. In this world those wearing a garment are more valuable than the garment. In the kingdom of the Heavens the garment is more valuable than the one wearing it.

28. By water and fire the entire realm is purified through the revelations by those who reveal them, and by the secrets through those who keep them. Yet, there are things kept secret

even within those things revealed. There is water in baptism and there is fire in the oil of anointing.

29. Jesus took them all by surprise. For he did not reveal himself as he originally was, but he revealed himself as they were capable of perceiving him. He revealed himself to all in their own way. To the great, he revealed himself as great. To the small he was small. He revealed himself to the angels as an angel and to mankind he was a man. Some looked at him and saw themselves. But, throughout all of this, he concealed his words from everyone. However when he revealed himself to his Disciples upon the mountain, he appeared glorious. He was not made small. He became great, but he also made the Disciples great so that they would be capable of comprehending his greatness.

30. He said on that day during his thanksgiving (in the Eucharist), "You have combined the perfect light and the holy spirit along with angels and images."

31. Do not hate the Lamb. Without him it is not possible to see the door to the sheepfold. Those who are naked will not come before the King.

32. The Sons of the Heavenly Man are more numerous than those of the earthly man. If the sons of Adam are numerous although they die, think of how many more Sons the Perfect Man has and these do not die. And they are continually born every instant of time.

33. The Father creates a son, but it is not possible for the son to create a son because it is impossible for someone who was just born to have a child. The Son has Brothers, not sons.

34. There is order in things. All those who are born in the world are begotten physically. Some are begotten spiritually, fed by the promise of heaven, which is delivered by the perfect Word from the mouth. The perfect Word is conceived through a kiss and thus they are born. There is unction to kiss one another to receive conception from grace to grace.

35. There were three women named Mary (Bitter) who walked with the Lord all the time. They were his mother, his sister and Mary of Magdala, who was his consort (companion). Thus his mother, his sister and companion (consort) were all named Mary.

36. "Father" and "Son" are single names, "Holy Spirit" is a double name and it is everywhere; above and below, secret and revealed. The Holy Spirit's abode is manifest when she is below. When she is above she is hidden.

37. Saints are served by evil powers (lesser gods). The evil spirits are deceived by the Holy Spirit. They think they are assisting a common man when they are serving Saints. A follower of the Lord once asked him for a thing from this world. He answered him saying, "Ask your Mother, and she will give you something from another realm."

38. The Apostles said to the students, "May all of our offering obtain salt!" They had called wisdom salt and without it no offering can become acceptable.

39. Wisdom (Sophia) is barren. She has no children but she is called Mother. Others are found (adopted) by the Holy Spirit, and she has many children.

40. That which the Father has belongs to the Son, but he cannot possess it when he is young (small). When he comes of age all his father has will be given to the son.

41. Those who do not follow the path are born of the Spirit, and they stray because of her. By this same spirit (breath or life force), the fire blazes and consumes.

42. Earthly wisdom is one thing, and death is another. Earthly wisdom is simply wisdom, but death is the wisdom of death, and death is the one who understands death. Being familiar with death is minor wisdom.

43. There are animals like the bull and donkey that are submissive to man. There are others that live in the wilderness. Man plows the field with submissive animals, and uses the harvest to feed himself as well as all the animals, domesticated or wild. So it is with the Perfect Man. Through submissive powers he plows and provides for all things to exist. He causes all things to come together into existence, whether good or evil, right or left.

44. The Holy Spirit is the shepherd guiding everyone and every power (lower ruler or lesser gods), whether submissive, rebellious, or feral. She controls them, subdues them, and keeps them bridled, whether they wish it or not.

45. Adam was created beautiful. One would expect his children to be noble. If he were not created but rather born, one would expect his children to be noble. But he was both created and born. Is this nobility?

46. Adultery occurred first and then came murder. And Cain was conceived in adultery because he was the serpent's (Satan's) son. He became a murderer just like his father. He killed his brother. When copulation occurs between those who are not alike, this is adultery.

47. God is a dyer. Just as a good and true dye penetrates deep into fabric to dye it permanently from within (not a surface act), so God has baptized what He dyes into an indelible dye, which is water.

48. It is impossible for anyone to see anything in the real world, unless he has become part of it. It is not like a person in this world. When one looks at the sun he can see it without being part of it. He can see the sky or the earth or anything without having to be part of it. So it is with this world, but in the other world you must become what you see (see what you become). To see spirit you must be spirit. To see Christ you must be Christ. To see the Father you must be the Father. In this way

you will see everything but yourself. If you look at yourself you will become what you see.

49. Faith receives, but love gives. No one can receive without faith. No one can love without giving. Believe and you shall receive. Love and you shall give. If you give without love, you shall receive nothing. Whoever has not received the Lord, continues to be a Jew.

50. The Apostles who came before us called him Jesus, The Nazarene, and The Messiah. Of these names, Jesus (Yeshua), The Nazarene (of the rite of the Nazarites), and The Messiah (Christ), the last name is the Christ, the first is Jesus, and the middle name is The Nazarene. Messiah has two meanings; the anointed one and the measured one. Jesus (Yeshua) means The Atonement (redemption or payment). 'Nazara' means Truth. Therefore, the Nazarite is The Truth. The Christ is The Measured One, the Nazarite (Truth) and Jesus (Redemption) have been measured (are the measurement).

51. The pearl which is thrown into the mud is not worth less than it was before. If it is anointed with balsam oil it is valued no higher. It is as valuable as its owner perceives it to be. So it

is with the children of God. Whatever becomes of them, they are precious in their Father's eyes.

52. If you say you are a Jew it will not upset anyone. If you say you are a Roman no one will care. If you claim to be a Greek, foreigner, slave, or a free man no one will be the least bit disturbed. But, if you claim to belong to Christ everyone will take heed (be concerned). I hope to receive this title from him. Those who are worldly would not be able to endure when they hear the name.

53. A god is a cannibal, because men are sacrificed to it. Before men were sacrificed, animals were sacrificed. Those they are sacrificed to are not gods.

54. Vessels of glass and vessels of clay are always made with fire. But if a glass vessel should break it is recast, because it is made in a single breath. If a clay vessel breaks it is destroyed, since it came into being without breath.

55. A donkey turning a millstone walked a hundred miles but when it was untied it was in the same place it started. There are those who go on long journeys but do not progress. When evening comes (when the journey ends), they have discovered

no city, no village, no construction site, no creature (natural thing), no power (ruler), and no angel. They labored and toiled for nothing (emptiness).

56. The thanksgiving (Eucharist) is Jesus. For in Aramaic they call him farisatha, which means, "to be spread out." This is because Jesus came to crucify the world.

57. The Lord went into the place where Levi worked as a dyer. He took 72 pigments and threw them into a vat. When he drew out the result it was pure white. He said, "This is how the Son of Man has come. He is a dyer."

58. Wisdom, which they call barren, is the mother of the angels. And the companion (Consort) was Mary of Magdala. The Lord loved Mary more than all the other disciples and he kissed her often on her mouth (the text is missing here and the word "mouth" is assumed). The others saw his love for Mary and asked him: "Why do you love her more than all of us?" The Savior replied, "Why do I not love you in the same way I love her?" While a blind person and a person who sees are both in the dark, there is no difference, but when the light comes, the one who sees shall behold the light, but he who is blind will remain in darkness.

59. The Lord says: "Blessed is he who existed before you came into being, for he is and was and shall (continue to) be."

60. The supremacy of man is not evident, but it is hidden. Because of this he is master of the animals, which are stronger (larger) than him, in ways both evident and not. This allows the animals to survive. But, when man departs from them, they bite and kill and devour each other because they have no food. Now they have food because man cultivated the land.

61. If one goes down into the water (is baptized) and comes up having received nothing, but claims to belong to Christ, he has borrowed against the name at a high interest rate. But if one receives the Holy Spirit, he has been given the name as a gift. He who has received a gift does not have to pay for it or give it back. If you have borrowed the name you will have to pay it back with interest when it is demanded. This is how the mystery works.

62. Marriage is a sacrament and a mystery. It is grand. For the world is founded upon man, and man founded upon marriage. Consider sex (pure sex), it has great power although its image is defiled.

63. Among the manifestations of unclean spirits there are male and female. The males are those who mate with the souls inhabiting a female form, and the female spirits invite those inhabiting a male form to have sex. Once seized, no one escapes unless they receive both the male and female power that is endued to the Groom with the Bride. The power is seen in the mirrored Bridal-Chamber. When foolish women see a man sitting alone, they want to subdue him, touch and handle him, and defile him. When foolish men see a beautiful woman sitting alone, they wish to seduce her, draw her in with desire and defile her. But, if the spirits see the man sitting together with his woman, the female spirit cannot intrude upon the man and the male spirit cannot intrude upon the woman. When image and angel are mated, no one can come between the man and woman.

64. He who comes out from the world cannot be stopped. Because he was once in the world he is now beyond both yearning (desire) and fear. He has overcome the flesh and has mastered envy and desire. If he does not leave the world there are forces that will come to seize him, strangle him. How can anyone escape? How can he fear them? Many times men will come and say, "We are faithful, and we hid from unclean and

demonic spirits." But if they had been given the Holy Spirit, no unclean spirit would have clung to them. Do not fear the flesh, nor love it. If you fear it, the flesh will become your master. If you love it, the flesh will devour you and render you unable to move.

65. One exists either in this world or in the resurrection or in transition between them. Do not be found in transition. In that world there is both good and evil. The good in it is not good and the evil in it is not evil. There is evil after this world, which is truly evil and it is called the transition. This is what is called death. While we are in this world it is best that we be born into the resurrection, so that we take off the flesh and find rest and not wander within the region of the transition. Many go astray along the way. Because of this, it is best to go forth from the world before one has sinned.

66. Some neither wish nor are able to act. Others have the will to act but it is best for them if they do not act, because the act they desire to perform would make them a sinner. By not desiring to do a righteous act justice is withheld (not obvious). However, the will always comes before the act.

67. An Apostle saw in a vision people confined to a blazing house, held fast in bonds of fire, crying out as flames came from their breath. There was water in the house, and they cried out, "The waters can truly save us." They were misled by their desire. This is called the outermost darkness.

68. Soul and spirit were born of water and fire. From water, fire, and light the children of the Bridal-Chamber are born. The fire is the spirit (anointing), the light is the fire, but not the kind of fire that has form. I speak of the other kind whose form is white and it rains down beauty and splendor.

69. The truth did not come into the world naked, but it came in types and symbols. The world would not receive it any other way. There is a rebirth together with its symbols. One cannot be reborn through symbols. What can the symbol of resurrection raise, or the Bridal-Chamber with its symbols? One must come into the truth through the (true) image (not the symbol or type of it). Truth is this Restoration. It is good for those not born to take on the names of the Father, the Son, and the Holy Spirit. They could not have done so on their own. Whoever is not born of them will have the name (Christ's ones) removed from him. The one who receives them receives the anointing of the spirit and the unction and power of the cross.

This is what the Apostles call having the right with the left. When this happens, you no longer belong to Christ, you will be Christ.

70. The Lord did everything through sacraments (mysteries or symbols): There was baptism, anointing, thanksgiving (Eucharist), atonement (sacrifice or payment), and Bridal-Chamber.

71. He says: "I came to make what is inside the same as the outside and what is below as it is above. I came to bring all of this into one place." He revealed himself through types and symbols. Those who say Christ comes from the place beyond (above) are confused.

72. He who is manifest in heaven is called "one from below." And He who knows the hidden thing is He who is above him. The correct way to say it would be "the inner and the outer or this which is beyond the outer." Because of this, the Lord called destruction "the outer darkness." There is nothing beyond it. He says, "My Father, who is in secret." He says, "Go into your inner chamber, shut the door behind you and there pray to your Father who is in secret; He who is deep within." He who is within them all is the Fullness. Beyond Him there is nothing

deeper within. The deepest place within is called the uppermost place.

73. Before Christ some came forth. They were not able to go back from where they came. They were no longer able to leave from where they went. Then Christ came. Those who went in he brought out, and those who went out he brought in.

74. When Eve was still within Adam (man), there had been no death. When she was separated from him, death began. If she were to enter him again and if he were to receive her completely, death would stop.

75. "My God, my God, Oh Lord why did you abandon me?" He spoke these words on the cross. He divided the place and was not there any longer.

76. The Lord arose from the dead. He became as he had been, but his body had been made perfect. He was clothed in true flesh. Our flesh is not true, but rather an image of true flesh, as one beholds in a mirror.

77. The Bridal-Chamber is not for beasts, slaves, or whores. It is for free men and virgins.

78. Through the Holy Spirit we are born again, conceived in Christ, anointed in the spirit, united within us. Only with light can we see ourselves reflected in water or mirror. We are baptized in water and light. It is the light that is the oil of the anointing.

79. There had been three offering vestibules in Jerusalem. One opened to the west called the holy, another opened to the south called the holy of the holy, the third opened to the east called the holy of the holies where the high priest alone was to enter. The Baptism is the holy, the redemption (payment or atonement) is the holy of the holy, and the holy of the holies is the Bridal-Chamber. The Baptism has within it the resurrection and the redemption. Redemption allows entrance into the Bridal-Chamber. The Bridal-Chamber is more exalted than any of these. Nothing compares.

80. Those who pray for Jerusalem love Jerusalem. They are in Jerusalem and they see it now. These are called the holy of the holies.

81. Before the curtain of the Temple was torn we could not see the Bridal-Chamber. All we had was the symbol of the place in

heaven. When the curtain was torn from the top to the bottom it made a way for some to ascend.

82. Those who have been clothed in the Perfect Light cannot be seen by the powers, nor can the powers subdue them. Yet one shall be clothed with light in the sacrament (mystery) of sex (being united).

83. If the woman had not been separated from the man, neither would have died. Christ came to rectify the error of separation that had occurred. He did this by re-uniting them and giving life to those who died. The woman unites with her husband in the Bridal-Chamber and those who have united in the Bridal-Chamber will not be parted again. Eve separated from Adam because she did not unite with him in the Bridal-Chamber.

84. The soul of man (Adam) was created when breath (spirit) was blown into him. The elements were supplied by his mother. When soul (mind or will) became spirit and were joined together he spoke in word the powers could not understand.

85. Jesus manifested beside the River Jordan with fullness of the kingdom of the Heavens, which existed before anything.

Moreover, he was born as a Son before birth. He was anointed and he anointed. He was atoned and he atoned.

86. It is right to speak of a mystery. The Father of them all mated with the Virgin who had come down. A fire shone over him on that day. He revealed the power of the Bridal-Chamber. Because of this power his body came into being on that day. He came forth in the Bridal-Chamber in glory because of the essence that issued forth from the Bridegroom to the Bride. This is how Jesus established everything. It was in his heart. In this same way it is right for each one of the disciples to enter into his rest.

87. Adam came into being from two virgins, from the Spirit and from the virgin earth. Christ was born from a virgin, so that the error which occurred in the beginning would be corrected by him.

88. There were two trees in paradise. One produced beasts, the other produced man. Adam ate from the tree that produced beasts becoming a beast he gave birth to beasts. Because of this, animals were worshipped. God created man and men created gods. This is how the world works; men create gods and they worship their creations. It would have been more appropriate

for gods to worship mankind. This would be the way if Adam had not eaten from the tree of life, which bore people.

89. The deeds of man follow his abilities. These are his strengths and the things he does with ease. His result is his children who came forth from his times of rest. His work is governed by his work but in his rest he brings forth his sons. This is the sign and symbol, doing works with strength, and producing children in his rest.

90. In this world the slaves are forced to serve the free. In the kingdom of Heaven the free shall serve the slaves and the Bridegroom of the Bridal-Chamber shall serve the guests. Those of the Bridal-Chamber have a single name among them, it is "rest" and they have no need for any other. The contemplation of the symbol brings enlightenment and great glory. Within those in the Chamber (rest) the glories are fulfilled.

91. Go into the water but do not go down into death, because Christ shall atone for him when he who is baptized comes forth. They were called to be fulfilled in his name. For he said, "We must fulfill all righteousness."

92. Those who say they shall die and then arise are confused. If you do not receive the resurrection while you are alive you will not receive anything when you die. This is why it is said that Baptism is great, because those who receive it shall live.

93. Philip the Apostle said, "Joseph the Carpenter planted a grove of trees because he needed wood for his work (craft or trade). He himself made the cross from the trees that he had planted, and his heir hung on that which he had planted. His heir was Jesus, and the tree was the cross. But the tree of life in the midst of the garden (paradise) is the olive tree. From the heart of it comes the anointing through the olive oil and from that comes the resurrection."

94. This world consumes corpses. Everything eaten by (in) the world dies. The truth devours life, but if you eat truth you shall never die. Jesus came (from there) bringing food. And to those wishing it (whom he wished) he gave life, so that they not die.

95. God created the garden (paradise). Man lived there, but they did not have God in their hearts and so they gave in to desire. This garden is where it will be said to us, " You may eat this but not eat that, according to your desire." This is the place where I shall choose to eat various things such as being there

the tree of knowledge, which slew Adam. In this place the tree of knowledge gave life to man. The Torah is the tree. It has the power to impart the knowledge of good and evil. It did not remove him from the evil or deliver him to good. It simply caused those who had eaten it to die. Death began because truth said, " You can eat this, but do not eat that."

96. The anointing (chrism) is made superior to Baptism, because from the word Chrism we are called Christians (Christ's ones) not because of the word Baptism. And because of Chrism he was called Christ. The Father anointed the Son, and the Son anointed the Apostles, and the Apostles anointed us. He who has been anointed has come to possess all things; he has the resurrection, the light, the cross, and the Holy Spirit. The Father bestowed this upon him in the Bridal-Chamber. The father gave it to the Son who received it freely. The Father was in the Son, and the Son was in the Father. This is the kingdom of Heaven.

97. It was perfectly said by the Lord: Some have attained the kingdom of Heaven laughing. They came forth from the world joyous. Those who belong to Christ who went down into the water immediately came up as lord of everything. He did not laugh because he took things lightly, but because he saw that

everything in this world was worthless compared to the kingdom of Heaven. If he scoffs at the world and sees its worthlessness he will come forth laughing.

98. The Bread and cup, and the oil of anointing (Chrism); there is one superior to them all.

99. The world (system) began in a mistake. He who made this world wished to make it perfect and eternal. He failed (fell away or did not follow through) and did not attain his goal. The world is not eternal, but the children of the world are eternal. They were children and obtained eternity. No one can receive eternity except by becoming a child. The more you are unable to receive, the more you will be unable to give.

100. The cup of the communion (prayer) contains wine and water. It is presented as the symbol of the blood. Over it (because of the blood) we give thanks. It is filled by (with) the Holy Spirit. It (the blood) belongs to the Perfect Man. When we drink we consume the Perfect man

101. The Living Water is a body. It is right that we be clothed with a living body (The Living Man). When he goes down into

the water he undresses himself so he may be clothed with the living man.

102. A horse naturally gives birth to a horse, a human naturally gives birth to a human, a god naturally gives birth to a god. The Bridegroom within the Bride gives birth to children who are born in the Bridal-Chamber. The Jews do not spring forth from Greeks (Gentiles), and Christians (those belonging to Christ) do not come from Jews. These who gave birth to Christians were called the chosen generation of the Holy Spirit (living God). The True Man, the Son of Mankind, was the seed that brought forth the sons of Man. This generation is the true ones in the world. This is the place where the children of the Bridal-Chamber dwell.

103. Copulation occurs in this world when man and woman mix (mingle or entwine). Strength joins with weakness. In eternity there is a different kind of mingling that occurs. Metaphorically we call it by the same names, but it is exalted beyond any name we may give it. It transcends brute strength. Where there is no force, there are those who are superior to force. Man cannot comprehend this.

104. The one is not, and the other one is, but they are united. This is He who shall not be able to come unto those who have a heart of flesh. (He is not here, but He exists. However, He cannot inhabit a heart of those who are attached to the fleshly world.)

105. Before you possess all knowledge, should you not know yourself? If you do not know yourself, how can you enjoy those things you have? Only those who have understood themselves shall enjoy the things they have come to possess.

106. The perfected person cannot be captured or seen. If they could see him, they could capture him. The path to grace can only come from the perfect light. Unless one is clothed in the perfect light and it shows on and in him he shall not be able to come out from the World as the perfected son of the Bridal-Chamber. We must be perfected before we come out from the world. Whoever has received all before mastering all, will not be able to master the kingdom. He shall go to the transition (death) imperfect. Only Jesus knows his destiny.

107. The holy person is entirely holy, including his body. If one blesses the bread and sanctifies it, or the cup, or everything else he receives, why will he not sanctify the body also?

108. By perfecting the water of Baptism: thus Jesus washed away death. Because of this, we are descended into the water but not into death. We are not poured out into the wind (spirit) of the world. Whenever that blows, its winter has come. When the Holy Spirit breathes, summer has come.

109. Whoever recognizes the truth is set free. He who is set free does not go back (sin), for the one who goes back (the sinner) is the slave of sin. Truth is the Mother. When we unite with her it is recognition of the truth. Those who are set free from sin (no longer have to sin) are called free by the world. It is the recognition of the truth that exalts the hearts of those who are set free from sin. This is what liberates them and places them over the entire world. Love builds (inspires). He who has been set free through this recognition is a slave of love, serving those who have not yet been set free by the truth. Knowledge makes them capable of being set free. Love does not take anything selfishly. How can it when it possesses all things? It does not say; "This is mine or that is mine," but it says, "All of this belongs to you."

110. Spiritual love is wine with fragrance. All those who are anointed with it enjoy it. Those who are near to the anointed

ones enjoy it also. But when the anointed ones depart the bystanders who are not anointed remain in their own stench. The Samaritan gave nothing to the wounded man except wine and oil for anointing. The wounds were healed, for "love covers a multitude of sins."

111. The children of a woman resemble the man who loves her. If the man is her husband, they resemble her husband. If the man is her illicit lover, they resemble him. Often, a woman will have sex with her husband out of duty but her heart is with her lover with whom she also has sex. The children of such a union often resemble the lover. You who live with the Son of God and do not also love the world but love the Lord only will have children that look like the Lord and not the world.

112. Humans mate with the humans, horses mate with horses, donkeys mate with donkeys. Like attracts like and they group together. Spirits unite with Spirits, and the thought (Word) mingles with the thought (Word), as Light merges with Light. If you become a person then people will love you. If you become a spirit, then the Spirit shall merge with you. If you become a thought, then the thought (Word) shall unite with you. If you become enlightened, then the Light shall merge with you. If you rise above this world, then that which is from

above shall rest upon (in) you. But, if you become like a horse, donkey, bull, dog, sheep, or any other animal, domestic or feral, then neither man nor Spirit nor Word (thought) nor the Light nor those from above nor those dwelling within shall be able to love you. They shall not be able to rest in you, and they will have no part in your inheritance to come.

113. He who is enslaved without his consent can be set free. He who has been set free by the grace of his master, but then sells himself back into slavery cannot be set free.

114. The cultivation in this world comes through four elements. Crops are harvested and taken into the barn only if there is first soil, water, wind, and light. God's harvest is also by means of four elements; faith (trust), hope (expectation), love (agape'), and knowledge (recognition of the truth). Our soil is the faith in which we take root. Our water is the hope by which we are nourished. Wind (spirit) is the love through which we grow. Light is the truth, which causes us to ripen. But, it is Grace that causes us to become kings of all heaven. Their souls are among the blessed for they live in Truth.

115. Jesus, the Christ, came to all of us but did not lay any burden on us. This kind of person is perfect and blessed. He is

the Word of God. Ask us about him and we will tell you his righteousness is difficult to define or describe. A task so great assures failure.

116. How will he give rest to everyone; great or small, believer or not? He provides rest to all. There are those who attempt to gain by assisting the rich. Those who see themselves as rich are picky. They do not come of their own accord. Do not grieve them or anyone. It is natural to want to do good, but understand that the rich may seek to cause grief and he who seeks to do good could annoy those who think they are rich.

117. A householder had acquired everything. He had children, slaves, cattle, dogs, and pigs. He also had wheat, barley, straw, hay, meat, oil, and acorns. He was wise and knew what each needed to eat. He fed his children bread and meat. He fed the slaves oil with grain. The cattle were given barley, straw and hay. The dogs received bones and the pigs got acorns and bread scraps. This is how it is with the disciple of God. If he is wise, he understands discipleship. The bodily forms will not deceive him, but he will understand the condition of the souls around him. He will speak to each man on his own level. In the world there are many types of animals in human form. He must recognize each one. If the person is a pig, feed him acorns.

If the person is a bull, feed him barley with straw and hay; if a dog, throw him bones. If a person is a slave feed him basic food, but to the sons present the perfect and complete food.

118. There is the Son of Man and there is the son of the son of Man. The Lord is the Son of Man, and his son creates through him. God gave the Son of Man the power to create; he also gave him the ability to have children. That which is created is a creature. Those born are a progeny (child or heir). A creature cannot propagate, but children can create. Yet they say that the creature procreates, however, the child is a creature. Therefore the creature's progeny are not his sons, but rather they are creations. He who creates works openly, and is visible. He who procreates does so in secret, and he hides himself from others. He who creates does so in open sight. He who procreates, makes his children (son) in secret.

119. No one is able to know what day a husband and wife copulate. Only they know, because marriage in this world is a sacrament (mystery) for those who have taken a wife. If the act of an impure (common) marriage is hidden, the pure (immaculate) marriage is a deeper mystery (sacrament) and is hidden even more. It is not carnal (common) but it is pure (undefiled). It is not founded on lust. It is founded on true love

(agape'). It is not part of the darkness or night. It is part of the light. A marriage (act) which is seen (revealed or exposed) becomes vulgarity (common or prostitution), and the bride has played the whore not only if she has sex with another man, but also if she escapes from the Bridal-Chamber and is seen. She may only be seen (reveal herself to) by her father, her mother, the attendant (friend) of the bridegroom, and the bridegroom. Only these have permission to go into the bridal-chamber on a daily basis. Others will yearn to hear her voice or enjoy her perfume (fragrance of the anointing oil). Let them be fed like dogs from the scraps that fall from the table. Those being from the Bridegroom with the Bride belong in the Bridal-Chamber. No one will be able to see the Bridegroom or the Bride unless he becomes one like (with) them.

120. When Abraham was allowed (rejoiced at seeing what he was) to see, he circumcised the flesh of the foreskin to show us that it was correct (necessary) to renounce (kill) the flesh of this world.

121. As long as the entrails of a person are contained, the person lives and is well. If his entrails are exposed and he is disemboweled, the person will die. It is the same with a tree. If its roots are covered it will live and grow, but if its roots are

exposed the tree will wither and die. It is the same with everything born into this world. It is this way with everything manifest (seen) and covert (unseen). As long as the roots of evil are hidden, it is strong, but once evil is exposed or recognized it is destroyed and it dies. This is why the Word says; "Already the ax has been laid to the root of the tree." It will not only chop down the tree, because that will permit it to sprout again, the ax will go down into the ground and cleave the very root. Jesus uprooted what others had only partially cut down. Let each one of us dig deeply, down to the root of the evil that is within his heart and rip it out by its roots. If we can just recognize evil we can uproot it. However, if evil remains unrecognized, it will take root within us and yield its fruit in our hearts. It will make evil our master and we will be its slaves. Evil takes us captive, and coerces us into doing what we do not want to do. Evil compels us into not doing what we should do. While it is unrecognized, it drives us .

122. Ignorance is the mother of all evil. Evil results in confusion and death. Truth is like ignorance. If it is hidden it rests within itself, but when it is revealed it is recognized and it is stronger than ignorance and error. Truth wins and liberates us from confusion. The Word said; "You shall know the truth and the truth shall set you free." Ignorance seeks to make us its slaves

but knowledge is freedom. By recognizing the truth, we shall find the fruits of the truth within our hearts. If we join ourselves with the truth we shall be fulfilled.

123. Now, we have the visible (beings) things of creation and we say that visible things (beings) are the powerful and honorable, but the invisible things are the weak and unworthy of our attention. The nature of truth is different. In it, the visible things (beings) are weak and lowly, but the invisible are the powerful and honorable. The wisdom of the invisible God cannot be made known to us except that he takes visible form in ways we are accustomed to. Yet the mysteries of the truth are revealed, in types and symbols, but the Bridal-Chamber is hidden as it is with the Holy of Holies.

124. The veil of the Temple first concealed how God governed creation. Once the veil was torn and the things within (the Holy of Holies) were revealed, the house was to be forsaken, abandoned, and destroyed. Yet the entire Divinity (Godhead) was to depart, not to the holies of the holies, for it was not able to merge with the light nor unite with the complete fullness. It was to be under the wings of the cross, in its open arms. This is the ark which shall be salvation for us when the destruction of water has overwhelmed (overtaken) them.

125. Those in the priestly tribe shall be able to enter within the veil of the Temple along with the High Priest. This was symbolized by the fact that the veil was not torn at the top only, (but was torn from top to the bottom). If it was torn only at the top it would have been opened only for those who are on high (from the higher realm). If it was torn at the bottom only it would have been revealed only to those who are from below (the lower realm). But it was torn from the top to the bottom. Those who are from above made it available to us who are below them, so that we might enter into the secret of the truth. This strengthening of us is most wonderful. Because of this, we can enter in by means of symbols even though they are weak and worthless. They are humble and incomplete when compared to the perfect glory. It is the glory of glories and the power of powers. Through it the perfect is opened to us and it contains the secrets of the truth. Moreover, the Holies of Holies have been revealed and opened, and the Bridal-Chamber has invited us in.

126. As long as evil is hidden, and not completely purged from among the children of the Holy Spirit, it remains a potential threat. The children can be enslaved by the adversary, but when the Perfect Light is seen, it will pour out the oil of

anointing upon and within it, and the slaves shall be set free and the slaves shall be bought back.

127. Every plant not sown by my heavenly Father shall be pulled up by the root. Those who were estranged shall be united and the empty shall be filled.

128. Everyone who enters the bridal-chamber shall ignite (be born in) the Light. This is like a marriage, which takes place at night. The fire is ablaze and is seen in the dark but goes out before morning. The mysteries (sacraments) of the marriage are consummated in the light of day, and that light never dies.

129. If someone becomes a child of the Bridal-Chamber, he shall receive the Light. If one does not receive it in this place, he will not be able to receive it in any other place. He who has received that Light shall not be seen, nor captured. No one in the world will be able to disturb him. When he leaves the world he will have already received the truth in types and symbols. The world has become eternity, because for him the fullness is eternal. It is revealed only to this kind of person. Truth is not hidden in darkness or the night. Truth is hidden in a perfect day and a holy light.

History of The Gospel Of Mary Magdalene

While traveling and researching in Cairo in 1896, German scholar, Dr. Carl Reinhardt, acquired a papyrus containing Coptic texts entitled the Revelation of John, the Wisdom of Jesus Christ, and the Gospel of Mary.

Before setting about to translate his exciting find two world wars ensued, delaying publication until 1955. By then the Nag Hammadi collection had also been discovered.

Two of the texts in his codex, the Revelation of John, and the Wisdom of Jesus Christ, were included there. Importantly, the codex preserves the most complete surviving copy of the Gospel of Mary, named for its supposed author, Mary of Magdala. Two other fragments of the Gospel of Mary written in Greek were later unearthed in archaeological digs at Oxyrhynchus in Northern Egypt.

All of the various fragments were brought together to form the translation presented here. However, even with all of the fragments assembled, the manuscript of the Gospel of Mary is missing pages 1 to 6 and pages 11 to 14. These pages included sections of the text up to chapter 4, and portions of chapter 5 to 8.

Although the text of the Gospel of Mary is incomplete, the text presented below serves to shake the very concept of our assumptions of early Christianity as well as Christ's possible relationship to Mary of Magdala, whom we call Mary Magdalene.

The Gospel of Mary Magdalene

(Pages 1 to 6, containing chapters 1 - 3, could not be recovered. The text starts on page 7, chapter 4)

Chapter 4

21 (And they asked Jesus), "Will matter then be destroyed or not?"

22) The Savior said, "All nature, all things formed, and all creatures exist in and with one another, and they will be dissolved again into their own elements (origins).

23) This is because it is the nature of matter to return to its original elements.

24) If you have an ear to hear, listen to this."

25) Peter said to him, "Since you have explained all things to us, tell us this also: What sin did the world commit (what sin is in the world)?"

26) The Savior said, "There is no sin (of the world). Each person makes his own sin when he does things like adultery (in the same nature as adultery). This is called sin.

27) That is why the Good came to be among you. He came to restore every nature to its basic root."

28) Then He continued; "You become sick and die because you did not have access to (knowledge of) Him who can heal you.

29) If you have any sense, you must understand this.

30) The material world produced a great passion (desire or suffering) without equal. This was contrary to the natural balance. The entire cosmos (body) was disturbed by it.

31) That is why I said to you, Be encouraged, and if you are discouraged be encouraged when you see the different forms nature has taken.

32) He who has ears to hear, let him hear."

33) When the Blessed One had said this, He greeted all of them and said; "Peace be with you. Take my peace into you.

34) Beware that no one deceives you by saying, 'Look (he is) here or look (he is) there. The Son of Man is within you.'

35) Follow Him there.

36) Those who seek Him will find Him.

37) Go now and preach the gospel (this good news) of the Kingdom.

38) Do not lay down any rules beyond what I told you, and do not give a law like the lawgivers (Pharisees) or you will be held to account for the same laws."

39) When He said this He departed.

Chapter 5

1) Then they were troubled and wept out loud, saying, "How shall we go to the Gentiles and preach the gospel of the Kingdom of the Son of Man? If they did not spare Him, how can we expect that they will spare us?"

2) Then Mary stood up, greeted them all, and said to her fellow believers, "Do not weep and do not be troubled and do not waver, because His grace will be with you completely and it will protect you.

3) Instead, let us praise His greatness, because He has prepared us and made us into mature (finished or complete) people."

4) Mary's words turned their hearts to the Good, and they began to discuss the words of the Savior.

5) Peter said to Mary, "Sister we know that the Savior loved you more than all other women.

6) Tell us the words of the Savior that you remember and know, but we have not heard and do not know."

7) Mary answered him and said, "I will tell you what He hid from you."

8) And she began to speak these words to them: She said, "I saw the Lord in a vision and I said to Him, 'Lord I saw you today in a vision.'

9) He answered and said to me; 'You will be happy that you did not waver at the sight of Me. Where the mind is there is the treasure.'

10) I said to Him; 'Lord, does one see visions through the soul or through the spirit?'

11) The Savior answered and said; 'He sees visions through neither the soul nor the spirit. It is through the mind that is between the two. That is what sees the vision and it is (there the vision exists).'"

(Pages 11 - 14 are missing. Text begins again at chapter 8)

Chapter 8

10) And Desire, (a lesser god), said, "Before, I did not see you descending, but now I see you ascending. Why do you lie since you belong to me?"

11) The soul answered and said, "I saw you but you did not see me nor recognize me. I covered you like a garment and you did not know me."

12) When it said this, the soul went away greatly rejoicing.

13) Again it came to the third power (lesser god), which is called Ignorance.

14) The power questioned the soul, saying, "Where are you going? You are enslaved (captured) in wickedness. Since you are its captive you cannot judge (have no judgment)."

15) And the soul said, "Why do you judge me, when I have not judged?"

16) "I was captured, although I have not captured anyone."

17) "I was not recognized. But I have recognized that God (the All) is in (being dissolved), both the earthly things and in the heavenly (things)."

18) When the soul had overcome the third power, it ascended and saw the fourth power, which took seven forms.

19) The first form is darkness, the second desire, the third ignorance, the fourth is the lust of death, the fifth is the dominion of the flesh, the sixth is the empty useless wisdom of flesh, the seventh is the wisdom of vengeance and anger. These are the seven powers of wrath.

20) They asked the soul, "Where do you come from, slayer of men: where are you going, conqueror of space?"

21) The soul answered and said, "What has trapped me has been slain, and what kept me caged has been overcome."

22) "My desire has been ended, and ignorance has died."

23) "In an age (dispensation) I was released from the world in a symbolic image, and I was released from the chains of oblivion, which were only temporary (in this transient world)."

24) "From this time on will I will attain the rest of the ages and seasons of silence."

Chapter 9

1) When Mary had said this, she fell silent, since she had shared all the Savior had told her.

2) But Andrew said to the other believers, "Say what you want about what she has said, but I do not believe that the Savior said this. These teachings are very strange ideas."

3) Peter answered him and spoke concerning these things.

4) He questioned them about the Savior and asked, "Did He really speak privately with a woman and not openly to us? Are we to turn around and all listen to her? Did He prefer her to us?"

5) Then Mary sobbed and said to Peter, "My brother Peter, what do you think? Do you think that I have made all of this up in my heart by myself? Do you think that I am lying about the Savior?"

6) Levi said to Peter, "Peter you have always had a hot temper.

7) Now I see you fighting against this woman like she was your enemy."

8) If the Savior made her worthy, who are you to reject her? What do you think you are doing? Surely the Savior knows her well?

9) That is why He loved her more than us. Let us be ashamed of this and let us put on the perfect Man. Let us separate from each other as He commanded us to do so we can preach the gospel, not laying down any other rule or other law beyond what the Savior told us."

10) And when they heard this they began to go out and proclaim and preach.

History of The Gospel of Thomas

In the winter of 1945, in Upper Egypt, an Arab peasant was gathering fertilizer and topsoil for his crops. While digging in the soft dirt he came across a large earthen vessel. Inside were scrolls containing hitherto unseen books.

According to local lore, the boy's father had recently been killed and the lad was preparing to chase the man who had murdered his father.

The scrolls were discovered near the site of the ancient town of Chenoboskion, at the base of a mountain named Gebel et-Tarif, near Hamra-Dum, in the vicinity of Naj 'Hammadi, about sixty miles from Luxor in Egypt. The texts were written in the Coptic language and preserved on papyrus sheets. The lettering style dated them as having been penned around the third or fourth century A.D. The Gospel of Thomas is the longest of the volumes consisting of 114 verses. Recent study indicates that the original work of Thomas, of which the scrolls are copies, may predate the four canonical gospels of Matthew, Mark, Luke, and John. The origin of The Gospel of Thomas is now thought to be from the first or second century A.D.

The word Coptic is an Arabic corruption of the Greek word Aigyptos, which in turn comes from the word Hikaptah, one of the names of the city of Memphis, the first capital of ancient Egypt.

There has never been a Coptic state or government per se, however the word has been used to generally define a culture and language present in the area of Egypt.

The known history of the Copts starts with King Mina the first King, who united the northern and southern kingdoms of Egypt circa 3050 B.C. The ancient Egyptian civilization under the rule of the Pharaohs lasted over 3000 years. Saint Mina (named after the king) is one of the major Coptic saints. He was martyred in 309 A.D.

The culture has come to be recognized as one containing distinctive art, architecture, and even a certain Christian church system.

The Coptic Church is based on the teachings of St. Mark, who introduced the region to Christianity in the first century A.D. The Copts take pride in the monastic flavor of their church and the fact that the Gospel of Mark is thought to be the oldest of the Gospels. Now, lying before a peasant boy was a scroll written in the ancient Coptic tongue: The Gospel of Thomas, possibly older than and certainly quite different from any other Gospel.

The peasant boy who found the treasure of the Gospel of Thomas stood to be rewarded greatly. This could have been the discovery of a lifetime for his family, but the boy had no idea what he had. He took the scrolls home, where his mother burned some as kindling.

Because the young man had succeeded in his pursuit of the father's murderer, he himself was now a murderer.

Fearing the authorities would soon come looking for him and not wanting to be found with ancient artifacts, he sold the codex to the black market antique dealers in Cairo for a trifle sum. It would be years until they found their way into the hands of a scholar.

Part of the thirteenth codex was smuggled from Egypt to America. In 1955 whispers of the existence of the codex had reached the ears of Gilles Quispel, a professor of religion and history in the Netherlands. The race was on to find and translate the scrolls.

The introduction of the collected sayings of Jesus refers to the writer as Didymos (Jude) Thomas. This is the same Thomas who doubted Jesus and was then told to place his hand within the breach in the side of the Savior. In the Gospel of St. John, he is referred to as Didymos, which means twin in Greek. In Aramaic, the name Jude (or Judas) also carries the sense of twin. The use of this title led some in the apocryphal tradition to believe that he was the twin brother and confidant of Jesus. However, when applied to Jesus himself, the literal meaning of twin must be rejected by orthodox Christianity as well as anyone adhering to the doctrine of the virgin birth of the only begotten Son of God. The title is likely meant to signify that Thomas was a close confidant of Jesus, or more simply, he was part of a set of twins and in no way related to Jesus.

Ancient church historians mention that Thomas preached to the Parthians in Persia and it is said he was buried in Edessa. Fourth century chronicles attribute the evangelization of India (Asia-Minor or Central Asia) to Thomas.

The text, which some believe predates the four gospels, has a very Eastern flavor. Since it is widely held that the four gospels of Matthew, Mark, Luke, and John have a common reference in the basic text of Mark, it stands to reason that all follow the same general history, insights, and language. Since scholars believe that the Gospel of Thomas predates the four main gospels, it can be assumed it was written outside the influences common to the other gospels.

The Gospel of Thomas is actually not a gospel at all. It contains no narrative but is instead a collection of sayings, which are said to be from Jesus himself as written (quoted) by Thomas. Although the codex found in Egypt is dated to the fourth century, most biblical scholars place the actual construction of the text of Thomas at about 70 – 150 A.D.

The gospel was often mentioned in early Christian literature, but no copy was thought to have survived until the discovery of the Coptic manuscript. Since then, part of the Oxyrynchus papyri have been identified as older Greek fragments of Thomas. The papyri were discovered in 1898 in the rubbish heaps of Oxyrhynchus, Egypt. This discovery yielded over thirty-five manuscript fragments for the New Testament. They have been dated to about 60 A.D. As a point of reference, a fragment of papyrus from the Dead Sea Scrolls had been dated to before 68 A.D.

There are marked differences between the Greek and Coptic texts, as we will see.

The debate on the date of Thomas centers in part on whether Thomas is dependent upon the canonical gospels, or is derived from an earlier document that was simply a collection of sayings. Many of the passages in Thomas appear to be more authentic versions of the synoptic parables, and many have parallels in Mark and Luke. This has caused a division of thought wherein some believe Thomas used common sources also used by Mark and Luke. Others believe Thomas was written independently after witnessing the same events.

If Thomas wrote his gospel first, without input from Mark, and from the standpoint of Eastern exposure as a result of his sojourn into India, it could explain the mystical quality of the text. It could also explain the striking differences in the recorded quotes of Jesus as memories were influenced by exposure to Asian culture.

There is some speculation that the sayings found in Thomas could be more accurate to the original intent and wording of Jesus than the other gospels. This may seem counter-intuitive until we realize that Christianity itself is an Eastern religion, albeit Middle-Eastern. Although as it spread west the faith went through many changes to westernize or Romanize it, Jesus was both mystical and Middle-Eastern. The Gospel of Thomas may not have seen as much "dilution" by Western society.

The Gospel of Thomas was most likely composed in Syria, where tradition holds that the church of Edessa was founded by Judas Thomas, The Twin (Didymos). The gospel may well be the earliest written tradition in the Syriac church.

The Gospel of Thomas is sometimes called a Gnostic gospel, although it seems more likely Thomas was adopted by the Gnostic community and interpreted in the light of their beliefs.

Gnostics believed that knowledge is formed or found from a personal encounter with God brought about by inward or intuitive insight. It is this knowledge that brings salvation. The Gnostics believed they were privy to a secret knowledge about the divine. It is their focus on knowledge that leads to their name.

The roots of the Gnosticism pre-date Christianity. Similarities exist to the wisdom and knowledge cults found in Egypt. The belief system seems to have spread and found a suitable home in the mystical side of the Christian faith.

There are numerous references to the Gnostics in second century literature. Their form of Christianity was considered heresy by the early church fathers. The intense resistance to the Gnostic belief system seems to be based in two areas. First, there was a general Gnostic belief that we were all gods, with heaven contained within us. Jesus, according to the Gnostics, was here to show us our potential to become as he was; a son or daughter of God, for God is both father and mother, male and female. These beliefs ran contrary to the newly developing orthodoxy. The second line of resistance was political. This resistance developed later and would have come from the fact that a faith based on a personal encounter flew in the face of the developing church political structure that placed priests and church as the keepers of heaven's gate with salvation through them alone.

It is from the writings condemning the group that we glean most of our information about the Gnostics. They are alluded to in the Bible in 1 Timothy 1:4 and 1 Timothy 6:20, and possibly the entirety of Jude, as the writers of the Bible defended their theology against that of the Gnostics.

The Coptic and Greek translations of The Gospel of Thomas presented herein are the result of a gestalt brought about by contrasting and comparing all of the foremost translations, where the best phrasing was chosen to follow the intent and meaning of the text.

Because there are differences between the Coptic manuscript and the Greek fragments of Thomas, each verse will have the following format for the reader to view: The Coptic text will be presented first, since we have the entire Gospel in this language. The Greek text will come next. If there is not a second rendition of the verse the reader may assume there was no Greek fragment found for that verse or the Greek version of the verse was identical to the Coptic version. Lastly, obvious parallels found in the Bible are listed.

Let us keep in mind that some of the differences between the translations of the Greek and Coptic may be attributed in part to the choice of word or phrase of those translating. It is the differences in overall meaning of verses between Coptic and Greek on which we should focus.

In the document to follow, the Gospel of Thomas will appear as a bold text. If there are other relevant but divergent interpretations of phrases in Thomas, they are included in parentheses. Any parallels of text or meaning that appear in the Bible are placed below the verse in italicized text. Author's notes are in regular text. In this way the reader can easily identify which body of work is being referenced and observe how they fit together.

Since the deeper meanings within Thomas are both in metaphor and in plain, understandable language, it is hoped that each time the words are read some new insight and treasure can be taken from them. As we change our perspective, we see the meaning of each verse differently. As one turns a single jewel to view each facet, we should study the Gospel of Thomas in the same way.

Let us begin.

The Gospel Of Thomas

These are the secret sayings which the living Jesus has spoken and Judas who is also Thomas (the twin) (Didymos Judas Thomas) wrote.

1. And he said: Whoever finds the interpretation of these sayings will not taste death.

1. He said to them: Whoever discovers the interpretation of these words shall never taste death.

John 8:51 Very truly I tell you, whoever keeps my word will never see death.

2. Jesus said: Let him who seeks not stop seeking until he finds, and when he finds he will be troubled, and when he has been troubled he will marvel (be astonished) and he will reign over all and in reigning, he will find rest.

2.   Jesus said: Let him who seeks not stop until he finds, and when he finds he shall wonder and in wondering he shall reign, and in reigning he shall find rest.

3.   Jesus said: If those who lead you say to you: Look, the Kingdom is in the sky, then the birds of the sky would enter before you. If they say to you: It is in the sea, then the fish of the sea would enter ahead you. But the Kingdom of God exists within you and it exists outside of you. Those who come to know (recognize) themselves will find it, and when you come to know yourselves you will become known and you will realize that you are the children of the Living Father. Yet if you do not come to know yourselves then you will dwell in poverty and it will be you who are that poverty.

3. Jesus said, If those who lead you say, "See, the Kingdom is in the sky," then the birds of the sky will precede you. If they say to you, "It is under the earth," then the fish of the sea will precede you. Rather, the Kingdom of God is inside of you, and it is outside of you.

Those who come to know themselves will find it; and when you come to know yourselves, you will understand that it is you who are the sons of the living Father. But if you will not

**know yourselves, you dwell in poverty and it is you who are
that poverty.**

Luke 17:20 And when he was demanded of by the Pharisees,
when the kingdom of God should come, he answered them and
said, The kingdom of God cometh not with observation:
Neither shall they say, Lo here! Lo there! For, behold, the
kingdom of God is within you.

**4. Jesus said: The person of old age will not hesitate to ask a
little child of seven days about the place of life, and he will
live. For many who are first will become last, (and the last
will be first). And they will become one and the same.**

**4.   Jesus said: Let the old man who has lived many days not
hesitate to ask the child of seven days about the place of life;
then he will live. For many that are first will be last, and last
will be first, and they will become a single one.**

*Mark 9:35-37 He sat down, called the twelve, and said to them:
Whoever wants to be first must be last of all and servant of all. Then
he took a little child and put it among them, and taking it in his arms,
he said to them: Whoever welcomes one such child in my name
welcomes me, and whoever welcomes me welcomes not me but the one
who sent me.*

5. Jesus said: Recognize what is in front of your face, and what has been hidden from you will be revealed to you. For there is nothing hidden which will not be revealed (become manifest), and nothing buried that will not be raised.

5.   Jesus said: Know what is in front of your face and what is hidden from you will be revealed to you.
For there is nothing hidden that will not be revealed.

Mark 4:2 For there is nothing hid, except to be made manifest; nor is anything secret, except it come to light.

Luke 12:3 Nothing is covered up that will not be revealed, or hidden that will not be known.

Matthew 10:26 So have no fear of them; for nothing is covered up that will not be uncovered, and nothing secret that will not become known.

6. His Disciples asked Him, they said to him: How do you want us to fast, and how will we pray? And how will we be charitable (give alms), and what laws of diet will we maintain?

Jesus said: Do not lie, and do not practice what you hate, for

everything is in the plain sight of Heaven. For there is nothing concealed that will not become manifest, and there is nothing covered that will not be exposed.

6.   His disciples asked him, "How do you want us to fast? And how shall we pray? And how shall we give alms? And what kind of diet shall we follow?"

Jesus said, don't lie, and don't do what you hate to do, for all things are revealed before the truth. For there is nothing hidden which shall not be revealed.

Luke 11:1 He was praying in a certain place, and after he had finished, one of his disciples said to him, Lord, teach us to pray, as John taught his disciples.

7. Jesus said: Blessed is the lion that the man will eat, for the lion will become the man. Cursed is the man that the lion shall eat, and still the lion will become man.

Mathew 26:20-30 He who dipped his hand with me in the dish, the same will betray me. The Son of Man goes, even as it is written of him, but woe to that man through whom the Son of Man is betrayed! It would be better for that man if he had not been born. Judas, who betrayed him, answered, "It isn't me, is it, Rabbi?" He said to him,

You said it. As they were eating, Jesus took bread, gave thanks for it, and broke it. He gave to the disciples, and said, Take, eat; this is my body. He took the cup, gave thanks, and gave to them, saying: All of you drink it, for this is my blood of the new covenant, which is poured out for many for the remission of sins. But I tell you that I will not drink of this fruit of the vine from now on, until that day when I drink it anew with you in my Father's Kingdom. When they had sung a hymn, they went out to the Mount of Olives.

8. And he said: The Kingdom of Heaven is like a wise fisherman who casts his net into the sea. He drew it up from the sea full of small fish. Among them he found a fine large fish. That wise fisherman threw all the small fish back into the sea and chose the large fish without hesitation. Whoever has ears to hear, let him hear!

Matthew 13:47-48 Again, the kingdom of heaven is like a net that was thrown into the sea and caught fish of every kind; when it was full, they drew it ashore, sat down, and put the good into baskets but threw out the bad.

9. Jesus said: Now, the sower came forth. He filled his hand and threw (the seeds). Some fell upon the road and the birds came and gathered them up. Others fell on the stone and they did not take deep enough roots in the soil, and so did not

produce grain. Others fell among the thorns and they choked the seed, and the worm ate them. Others fell upon the good earth and it produced good fruit up toward the sky, it bore 60 fold and 120 fold.

Matthew 13:3-8 And he told them many things in parables, saying: Listen! A sower went out to sow. And as he sowed, some seeds fell on the path, and the birds came and ate them up. Other seeds fell on rocky ground, where they did not have much soil, and they sprang up quickly, since they had no depth of soil. But when the sun rose, they were scorched; and since they had no root, they withered away. Other seeds fell among thorns, and the thorns grew up and choked them. Other seeds fell on good soil and brought forth grain, some a hundred fold, some sixty, some thirty.

Mark 4:2-9 And he taught them many things in parables, and in his teaching he said to them: Behold! A sower went out to sow. And as he sowed, some seed fell along the path, and the birds came and devoured it. Other seed fell on rocky ground, where it had not much soil, and immediately it sprang up, since it had no depth of soil; and when the sun rose it was scorched, and since it had no root it withered away. Other seed fell among thorns and the thorns grew up and choked it, and it yielded no grain. And other seeds fell into good soil and brought forth grain, growing up and increasing and yielding thirty fold and sixty fold and a hundred fold. And he said, He who has ears to hear, let him hear.

Luke 8:4-8 And when a great crowd came together and people from town after town came to him, he said in a parable: A sower went out to sow his seed; and as he sowed, some fell along the path, and was trodden under foot, and the birds of the air devoured it. And some fell on the rock; and as it grew up, it withered away, because it had no moisture. And some fell among thorns; and the thorns grew with it and choked it. And some fell into good soil and grew, and yielded a hundred fold. As he said this, he called out, He who has ears to hear, let him hear.

10. Jesus said: I have cast fire upon the world, and as you see, I guard it until it is ablaze.

Luke 12:49 I came to bring fire to the earth, and how I wish it were already kindled.

11. Jesus said: This sky will pass away, and the one above it will pass away. The dead are not alive, and the living will not die. In the days when you consumed what is dead, you made it alive. When you come into the Light, what will you do? On the day when you were united (one), you became separated (two). When you have become separated (two), what will you

do?

Matthew 24:35 Heaven and earth will pass away, but my words will not pass away.

12. The Disciples said to Jesus: We know that you will go away from us. Who is it that will be our teacher?

Jesus said to them: Wherever you are (in the place that you have come), you will go to James the Righteous, for whose sake Heaven and Earth were made (came into being.)

13. Jesus said to his Disciples: Compare me to others, and tell me who I am like. Simon Peter said to him: You are like a righteous messenger (angel) of God. Matthew said to him: You are like a (wise) philosopher (of the heart). Thomas said to him: Teacher, my mouth is not capable of saying who you are like!

Jesus said: I'm not your teacher, now that you have drunk; you have become drunk from the bubbling spring that I have tended (measured out). And he took him, and withdrew and spoke three words to him: ahyh ashr ahyh (I am who I am).

Now when Thomas returned to his comrades, they inquired of him: What did Jesus say to you? Thomas said to them: If I tell you even one of the words which he spoke to me, you will take up stones and throw them at me, and fire will come from the stones to consume you.

Mark 8:27-30 Jesus went on with his disciples to the villages of Caesarea Philippi; and on the way he asked his disciples, Who do people say that I am? And they answered him, John the Baptist; and others, Elijah; and still others, one of the prophets. He asked them, But who do you say that I am? Peter answered him, You are the Messiah. And he sternly ordered them not to tell anyone about him.

14. Jesus said to them: If you fast, you will give rise to transgression (sin) for yourselves. And if you pray, you will be condemned. And if you give alms, you will cause harm (evil) to your spirits. And when you go into the countryside, if they take you in (receive you) then eat what they set before you and heal the sick among them. For what goes into your mouth will not defile you, but rather what comes out of your mouth, that is what will defile you.

Luke 10:8-9 Whenever you enter a town and its people welcome you, eat what is set before you; Cure the sick who are there, and say to them, The kingdom of God has come near to you.

Mark 7:15 There is nothing outside a person that by going in can defile, but the things that come out are what defile.

Matthew 15:11 It is not what goes into the mouth that defiles a man, but what comes out of the mouth, this defiles a man.

Romans 14.14 I know and am persuaded in the Lord Jesus that nothing is unclean in itself; but it is unclean for any one who thinks it unclean.

15. Jesus said: When you see him who was not born of woman, bow yourselves down upon your faces and worship him for he is your Father.

Galatians 4:3-5 Even so we, when we were children, were in bondage under the elements of the world: But when the fullness of the time was come, God sent forth his Son, made of a woman, made under the law, To redeem them that were under the law, that we might receive the adoption of sons.

16. Jesus said: People think perhaps I have come to spread peace upon the world. They do not know that I have come to

cast dissention (conflict) upon the earth; fire, sword, war. For there will be five in a house. Three will be against two and two against three, the father against the son and the son against the father. And they will stand alone.

Matthew 10:34-36 Do not think that I have come to bring peace to the earth; I have not come to bring peace, but a sword. For I have come to set a man against his father, and a daughter against her mother, and a daughter-in-law against her mother-in-law; and one's foes will be members of one's own household.

Luke 12:51-53 Do you think that I have come to give peace on earth? No, I tell you, but rather division; for henceforth in one house there will be five divided, three against two and two against three; they will be divided, father against son and son against father, mother against daughter and daughter against her mother, mother-in-law against her daughter-in-law and daughter-in-law against her mother-in-law.

17. Jesus said: I will give to you what eye has not seen, what ear has not heard, what hand has not touched, and what has not occurred to the mind of man.

1 Cor 2:9 But, as it is written, What no eye has seen, nor ear heard, nor the human heart conceived, what God has prepared for those who love him.

18. The Disciples said to Jesus: Tell us how our end will come. Jesus said: Have you already discovered the beginning (Origin), so that you inquire about the end? Where the beginning (origin) is, there the end will be. Blessed be he who will take his place in the beginning (stand at the origin) for he will know the end, and he will not experience death.

19. Jesus said: Blessed is he who came into being before he came into being. If you become my Disciples and heed my sayings, these stones will serve you. For there are five trees in paradise for you, which are undisturbed in summer and in winter and their leaves do not fall. Whoever knows them will not experience death.

20. The Disciples said to Jesus: Tell us what the Kingdom of Heaven is like. He said to them: It is like a mustard seed, smaller than all other seeds and yet when it falls on the tilled earth, it produces a great plant and becomes shelter for the birds of the sky.

Mark 4:30-32 He also said, With what can we compare the kingdom of God, or what parable will we use for it? It is like a mustard seed, which, when sown upon the ground, is the smallest of all the seeds on earth; yet when it is sown it grows up and becomes the greatest of all shrubs, and puts forth large branches, so that the birds of the air can make nests in its shade.

Matthew 13:31-32 The kingdom of heaven is like a grain of mustard seed which a man took and sowed in his field; it is the smallest of all seeds, but when it has grown it is the greatest of shrubs and becomes a tree, so that the birds of the air come and make nests in its branches.

Luke 13.18-19 He said therefore, What is the kingdom of God like? And to what shall I compare it? It is like a grain of mustard seed which a man took and sowed in his garden; and it grew and became a tree, and the birds of the air made nests in its branches.

21. Mary said to Jesus: Who are your Disciples like? He said: They are like little children who are living in a field that is not theirs. When the owners of the field come, they will say: Let us have our field! It is as if they were naked in front of them (They undress in front of them in order to let them have what is theirs) and they give back the field. Therefore I say, if the owner of the house knows that the thief is coming, he will be alert before he arrives and will not allow him to dig

through into the house to carry away his belongings. You, must be on guard and beware of the world (system). Prepare yourself (arm yourself) with great strength or the bandits will find a way to reach you, for the problems you expect will come. Let there be among you a person of understanding (awareness). When the crop ripened, he came quickly with his sickle in his hand to reap. Whoever has ears to hear, let him hear!

Matthew 24:43 But understand this: if the owner of the house had known in what part of the night the thief was coming, he would have stayed awake and would not have let his house be broken into.

Mark 4:26-29 He also said, The kingdom of God is as if someone would scatter seed on the ground, and would sleep and rise night and day, and the seed would sprout and grow, he does not know how. The earth produces of itself, first the stalk, then the head, then the full grain in the head. But when the grain is ripe, at once he goes in with his sickle, because the harvest has come.

Luke 12:39-40 But know this, that if the householder had known at what hour the thief was coming, he would not have left his house to be broken into. You also must be ready; for the Son of man is coming at an unexpected hour.

22. Jesus saw little children who were being suckled. He said to his Disciples: These little children who are being suckled are like those who enter the Kingdom.

They said to him: Should we become like little children in order to enter the Kingdom?

Jesus said to them: When you make the two one, and you make the inside as the outside and the outside as the inside, when you make the above as the below, and if you make the male and the female one and the same (united male and female) so that the man will not be masculine (male) and the female be not feminine (female), when you establish an eye in the place of an eye and a hand in the place of a hand and a foot in the place of a foot and a likeness (image) in the place of a likeness (an image), then will you enter the Kingdom.

Luke 18:16 But Jesus called for them and said, Let the little children come to me, and do not stop them; for it is to such as these that the kingdom of God belongs. Truly I tell you, whoever does not receive the kingdom of God as a little child will never enter it.

Mark 9:43-48 If your hand causes you to stumble, cut it off; it is better for you to enter life maimed than to have two hands and to go to hell, to the unquenchable fire. And if your foot causes you to stumble, cut it off; it is better for you to enter life lame than to have two feet and to be thrown into hell. And if your eye causes you to stumble, tear it out; it is better for you to enter the kingdom of God with one eye than to have two eyes and to be thrown into hell, where the worm never dies, and the fire is never quenched.

Matthew 18:3-5 And said, Verily, I say unto you, unless you turn and become like children, you will never enter the kingdom of heaven. Whoever humbles himself like this child, he is the greatest in the kingdom of heaven. Whoever receives one such child in my name receives me;

Matthew 5:29-30 If your right eye causes you to sin, pluck it out and throw it away; it is better that you lose one of your members than that your whole body be thrown into hell. And if your right hand causes you to sin, cut it off and throw it away; it is better that you lose one of your members than that your whole body go into hell.

23. Jesus said: I will choose you, one out of a thousand and two out of ten thousand and they will stand as a single one.

Matthew 20:16 So the last shall be first, and the first last: for many be called, but few chosen.

24. His Disciples said: Show us the place where you are (your place), for it is necessary for us to seek it.

24. He said to them: Whoever has ears, let him hear! Within a man of light there is light, and he illumines the entire world. If he does not shine, he is darkness (there is darkness).

John13:36 Simon Peter said to him, Lord, where are you going? Jesus answered, Where I am going, you cannot follow me now; but you will follow afterward.

Matthew 6:22-23 The eye is the lamp of the body. So, if your eye is healthy, your whole body will be full of light; but if your eye is unhealthy, your whole body will be full of darkness. If then the light in you is darkness, how great is the darkness!

Luke 11:34-36 Your eye is the lamp of your body; when your eye is sound, your whole body is full of light; but when it is not sound, your body is full of darkness. Therefore be careful lest the light in you be darkness. If then your whole body is full of light, having no part dark, it will be wholly bright, as when a lamp with its rays gives you light.

Author's Note:

Early philosophers thought that light was transmitted from the eye and bounced back, allowing the person to sense the world at large. Ancient myths tell of Aphrodite constructing the human eye out of the four elements (earth, wind, fire, and water). The eye was held together by love. She kindled the fire of the soul and used it to project from the eyes so that it would act like a lantern, transmitting the light, thus allowing us to see.

Euclid, (330 BC to 260BC) speculated about the speed of light being instantaneous since you close your eyes, then open them again; even the distant objects appear immediately.

25. Jesus said: Love your friend (Brother) as your soul; protect him as you would the pupil of your own eye.

Romans 12:9-11 Let love be without dissimulation. Abhor that which is evil; cleave to that which is good. Be kindly affectioned one to another with brotherly love; in honour preferring one another; Not slothful in business; fervent in spirit; serving the Lord...

26. Jesus said: You see the speck in your brother's eye but the beam that is in your own eye you do not see. When you

remove the beam out of your own eye, then will you see clearly to remove the speck out of your brother's eye.

26. Jesus said, You see the splinter in your brother's eye, but you don't see the log in your own eye. When you take the log out of your own eye, then you will see well enough to remove the splinter from your brother's eye.

Matthew 7:3-5 Why do you see the speck in your neighbor's eye, but do not notice the log in your own eye? Or how can you say to your neighbor, Let me take the speck out of your eye, while the log is in your own eye? You hypocrite, first take the log out of your own eye, and then you will see clearly to take the speck out of your neighbor's eye.

Luke 6:41-42 Why do you see the speck that is in your brother's eye, but do not notice the log that is in your own eye? Or how can you say to your brother, Brother, let me take out the speck that is in your eye, when you yourself do not see the log that is in your own eye? You hypocrite, first take the log out of your own eye, and then you will see clearly to take out the speck that is in your brother's eye.

27. Jesus said: Unless you fast from the world (system), you will not find the Kingdom of God. Unless you keep the

Sabbath (entire week) as Sabbath, you will not see the Father.

27. Jesus said: Unless you fast (abstain) from the world, you shall in no way find the Kingdom of God; and unless you observe the Sabbath as a Sabbath, you shall not see the Father.

28. Jesus said: I stood in the midst of the world. In the flesh I appeared to them. I found them all drunk; I found none thirsty among them. My soul grieved for the sons of men, for they are blind in their hearts and do not see that they came into the world empty they are destined (determined) to leave the world empty. However, now they are drunk. When they have shaken off their wine, then they will repent (change their ways).

28. Jesus said: I took my stand in the midst of the world, and they saw me in the flesh, and I found they were all drunk, and I found none of them were thirsty. And my soul grieved over the souls of men because they are blind in their hearts. They do not see that they came into the world empty, therefore they are determined to leave the world empty. However, now they are drunk. When they have shaken off their wine, then they will change their ways.

29. Jesus said: If the flesh came into being because of spirit, it is a marvel, but if spirit came into being because of the body, it would be a marvel of marvels. I marvel indeed at how great wealth has taken up residence in this poverty.

30. Jesus said: Where there are three gods, they are gods (Where there are three gods they are without god). Where there is only one, I say that I am with him. Lift the stone and there you will find me, Split the wood and there am I.

30. Jesus said: Where three are together they are not without God, and when there is one alone, I say, I am with him.

Author's Note:
Many scholars believe pages of the manuscript were misplaced and verses 30 and 77 should run together as a single verse.

77. Jesus said: I-Am the Light who is over all things, I-Am the All. From me all came forth and to me all return (The All came from me and the All has come to me). Split wood, there am I. Lift up the stone and there you will find me.

Matthew 18:20 For where two or three are gathered in my name, I am there among them.

31. Jesus said: No prophet is accepted in his own village, no physician heals those who know him.

31. Jesus said: A prophet is not accepted in his own country, neither can a doctor cure those that know him.

Mark 6:4 Then Jesus said to them, Prophets are not without honor, except in their hometown, and among their own kin, and in their own house.

Matthew 13:57 And they took offense at him. But Jesus said to them: A prophet is not without honor save in his own country and in his own house.

Luke 4:24 And he said, Truly, I say to you, no prophet is acceptable in his own country.

John 4:43-44 After the two days he departed to Galilee. For Jesus himself testified that a prophet has no honor in his own country.

32. Jesus said: A city being built (and established) upon a high mountain and fortified cannot fall nor can it be hidden.

107

32. Jesus said: A city built on a high hilltop and fortified can neither fall nor be hidden.

Matthew 5:14 You are the light of the world. A city built on a hill cannot be hid.

33. Jesus said: What you will hear in your ear preach from your rooftops. For no one lights a lamp and sets it under a basket nor puts it in a hidden place, but rather it is placed on a lamp stand so that everyone who comes and goes will see its light.

33. Jesus said: What you hear with one ear preach from your rooftops. For no one lights a lamp and sets it under a basket or hides, but rather it is placed on a lamp stand so that everyone who comes and goes will see its light.

Matthew 10:27 What I say to you in the dark, tell in the light; and what you hear whispered, proclaim from the housetops.

Luke 8:16 No one after lighting a lamp hides it under a jar, or puts it under a bed, but puts it on a lamp stand, so that those who enter may see the light.

Matthew 5:15 Nor do men light a lamp and put it under a bushel, but on a stand, and it gives light to all in the house.

Mark 4:21 And he said to them, Is a lamp brought in to be put under a bushel, or under a bed, and not on a stand?

Luke 11:33 No one after lighting a lamp puts it in a cellar or under a bushel, but on a stand, that those who enter may see the light.

34. Jesus said: If a blind person leads a blind person, both fall into a pit.

Matthew 15:14 Let them alone; they are blind guides of the blind. And if one blind person guides another, both will fall into a pit.

Luke 6:39 He also told them a parable: Can a blind man lead a blind man? Will they not both fall into a pit?

35. Jesus said: It is impossible for anyone to enter the house of a strong man to take it by force unless he binds his hands, then he will be able to loot his house.

Matthew 12:29 Or how can one enter a strong man's house and plunder his goods, unless he first binds the strong man? Then indeed he may plunder his house.

Luke 11:21-22 When a strong man, fully armed, guards his own palace, his goods are in peace; but when one stronger than he assails him and overcomes him, he takes away his armor in which he trusted, and divides his spoil.

Mark 3:27 But no one can enter a strong man's house and plunder his property without first tying up the strong man; then indeed the house can be plundered.

36. Jesus said: Do not worry from morning to evening nor from evening to morning about the food that you will eat nor about what clothes you will wear. You are much superior to the Lilies which neither card nor spin. When you have no clothing, what do you wear? Who can add time to your life (increase your stature)? He himself will give to you your garment.

Matthew 6:25-31 Therefore I tell you, do not worry about your life, what you will eat or what you will drink, or about your body, what you will wear. Is not life more than food, and the body more than clothing? Look at the birds of the air; they neither sow nor reap nor gather into barns, and yet your heavenly Father feeds them. Are you not of more value than they? And can any of you by worrying add a single hour to your span of life? And why do you worry about clothing? Consider the lilies of the field, how they grow; they neither toil nor spin, yet I tell you, even Solomon in all his glory was not clothed like one of these. But if God so clothes the grass of the field, which is alive today and tomorrow is thrown into the oven, will he not much more clothe you--you of little faith? Therefore do not worry, saying, What will we eat? or What will we drink? or What will we wear?

Luke 12:22-23 And he said to his disciples, Therefore I tell you, do not be anxious about your life, what you shall eat, nor about your body, what you shall put on. For life is more than food, and the body more than clothing.

37. His Disciples said: When will you appear to us, and when will we see you?

Jesus said: When you take off your garments without being ashamed, and place your garments under your feet and tread on them as the little children do, then will you see the Son of the Living-One, and you will not be afraid.

37 His disciples said to him, when will you be visible to us, and when shall we be able to see you?

He said, when you strip naked without being ashamed and place your garments under your feet and tread on them as the

little children do, then will you see the Son of the Living-One, and you will not be afraid.

38. Jesus said: Many times have you yearned to hear these sayings which I speak to you, and you have no one else from whom to hear them. There will be days when you will seek me but you will not find me.

39. Jesus said: The Pharisees and the Scribes have received the keys of knowledge, but they have hidden them. They did not go in, nor did they permit those who wished to enter to do so. However, you be as wise (astute) as serpents and innocent as doves.

39. Jesus said: The Pharisees and the Scribes have stolen the keys of heaven, but they have hidden them. They have entered in, but they did not permit those who wished to enter to do so. However, you be as wise as serpents and innocent as doves.

Luke 11:52 Woe to you lawyers! For you have taken away the key of knowledge; you did not enter yourselves, and you hindered those who were entering.

Matthew 10:16 See, I am sending you out like sheep into the midst of wolves; so be wise as serpents and innocent as doves.

Matthew 23.13 But woe unto you, scribes and Pharisees, hypocrites! because you shut the kingdom of heaven against men; for you neither enter yourselves, nor allow those who would enter to go in.

40. Jesus said: A grapevine has been planted outside the (vineyard of the) Father, and since it is not viable (supported) it will be pulled up by its roots and destroyed.

Matthew 15:13 He answered, Every plant that my heavenly Father has not planted will be uprooted.

41. Jesus said: Whoever has (it) in his hand, to him will (more) be given. And whoever does not have, from him will be taken even the small amount which he has.

Matthew 25:29 For to all those who have, more will be given, and they will have an abundance; but from those who have nothing, even what they have will be taken away.

Luke 19:26 I tell you, that to every one who has will more be given; but from him who has not, even what he has will be taken away.

42. Jesus said: Become passers-by.

43. His Disciples said to him: Who are you, that you said these things to us?

Jesus said to them: You do not recognize who I am from what I said to you, but rather you have become like the Jews who either love the tree and hate its fruit, or love the fruit and hate the tree.

John 8:25 They said to him, Who are you? Jesus said to them, Why do I speak to you at all?

Matthew 7:16-20 You will know them by their fruits. Are grapes gathered from thorns, or figs from thistles? In the same way, every good tree bears good fruit, but the bad tree bears bad fruit. A good tree cannot bear bad fruit, nor can a bad tree bear good fruit. Every tree that does not bear good fruit is cut down and thrown into the fire. Thus you will know them by their fruits.

44. Jesus said: Whoever blasphemes against the Father, it will be forgiven him. And whoever blasphemes against the Son, it will be forgiven him. Yet whoever blasphemes against the Holy Spirit, it will not be forgiven him neither on earth nor in heaven.

Mark 3:28-29 Truly I tell you, people will be forgiven for their sins and whatever blasphemies they utter; but whoever blasphemes against the Holy Spirit can never have forgiveness, but is guilty of an eternal sin.

Matthew 12:31-32 Therefore I tell you, every sin and blasphemy will be forgiven men, but the blasphemy against the Spirit will not be forgiven. And whoever says a word against the Son of man will be forgiven; but whoever speaks against the Holy Spirit will not be forgiven, either in this age or in the age to come.

Luke 12:10 And every one who speaks a word against the Son of man will be forgiven him; but he who blasphemes against the Holy Spirit will not be forgiven.

45. Jesus said: Grapes are not harvested from thorns, nor are figs gathered from thistles, for they do not give fruit. A good person brings forth goodness out of his storehouse. A bad person brings forth evil out of his evil storehouse which is in his heart, and he speaks evil, for out of the abundance of the heart he brings forth evil.

Luke 6:43-45 For no good tree bears bad fruit, nor again does a bad tree bear good fruit; for each tree is known by its own fruit. For figs are not gathered from thorns, nor are grapes picked from a bramble bush. *The good man out of the good treasure of his heart produces good, and the evil man out of his evil treasure produces evil; for out of the abundance of the heart his mouth speaks.*

46. Jesus said: From Adam until John the Baptist there is none born of women who surpasses John the Baptist, so that his eyes should not be downcast (lowered). Yet I have said that whoever among you becomes like a child will know the Kingdom, and he will be greater than John.

Matthew 11:11 Truly I tell you, among those born of women no one has arisen greater than John the Baptist; yet the least in the kingdom of heaven is greater than he.

Luke 7:28 I tell you, among those born of women none is greater than John; yet he who is least in the kingdom of God is greater than he.

Matthew 18:2-4 He called a child, whom he put among them, and said, Truly I tell you, unless you change and become like children, you will never enter the kingdom of heaven. Whoever becomes humble like this child is the greatest in the kingdom of heaven.

47. Jesus said: It is impossible for a man to mount two horses or to draw two bows, and a servant cannot serve two masters, otherwise he will honor the one and disrespect the other. No

man drinks vintage wine and immediately desires to drink new wine, and they do not put new wine into old wineskins or they would burst, and they do not put vintage wine into new wineskins or it would spoil (sour). They do not sew an old patch on a new garment because that would cause a split.

Matthew 6:24 No one can serve two masters; for a slave will either hate the one and love the other, or be devoted to the one and despise the other. You cannot serve God and wealth.

Matthew 9:16-17 No one sews a piece of cloth, not yet shrunk, on an old cloak, for the patch pulls away from the cloak, and a worse tear is made. Neither is new wine put into old wineskins; otherwise, the skins burst, and the wine is spilled, and the skins are destroyed; but new wine is put into fresh wineskins, and so both are preserved.

Mark 2:21-22 No one sews a piece of unshrunk cloth on an old garment; if he does, the patch tears away from it, the new from the old, and a worse tear is made. And no one puts new wine into old wineskins; if he does, the wine will burst the skins, and the wine is lost, and so are the skins; but new wine is for fresh skins.

Luke 5:36-39 He told them a parable also: No one tears a piece from a new garment and puts it upon an old garment; if he does, he will tear the new, and the piece from the new will not match the old. And no one puts new wine into old wineskins; if he does, the new wine will burst the skins and it will be spilled, and the skins will be destroyed. But new wine must be put into fresh wineskins. And no one after drinking old wine desires new; for he says, "The old is good."

48. Jesus said: If two make peace with each other in this one house, they will say to the mountain: Be moved! and it will be moved.

Matthew 18:19 Again, truly I tell you, if two of you agree on earth about anything you ask, it will be done for you by my Father in heaven.

Mark 11:23-24 Truly I tell you, if you say to this mountain, Be taken up and thrown into the sea, and if you do not doubt in your heart, but believe that what you say will come to pass, it will be done for you. So I tell you, whatever you ask for in prayer, believe that you have received it, and it will be yours.

Matthew 17:20 He said to them, Because of your little faith. For truly, I say to you, if you have faith as a grain of mustard seed, you will say to this mountain, Move from here to there, and it will move; and nothing will be impossible to you.

49. Jesus said: Blessed is the solitary and chosen, for you will find the Kingdom. You have come from it, and unto it you

will return.

Matthew 5:1-3 And seeing the multitudes, he went up into a mountain: and when he was set, his disciples came unto him: And he opened his mouth, and taught them, saying, Blessed are the poor in spirit: for theirs is the kingdom of heaven.

John 20:28-30 And Thomas answered and said unto him, My LORD and my God. Jesus saith unto him, Thomas, because thou hast seen me, thou hast believed: blessed are they that have not seen, and yet have believed. And many other signs truly did Jesus in the presence of his disciples, which are not written in this book:

50. Jesus said: If they say to you: From where do you come? Say to them: We have come from the Light, the place where the Light came into existence of its own accord and he stood and appeared in their image. If they say to you: Is it you? (Who are you?), say: We are his Sons and we are the chosen of the Living Father. If they ask you: What is the sign of your Father in you? Say to them: It is movement with rest (peace in the midst of motion or chaos).

51. His Disciples said to him: When will the rest of the dead occur, and when will the New World come? He said to them:

That which you look for has already come, but you do not recognize it.

52. His Disciples said to him: Twenty-four prophets preached in Israel, and they all spoke of you (in your spirit). He said to them: You have ignored the Living-One who is in your presence and you have spoken only of the dead.

53. His Disciples said to him: Is circumcision beneficial or not? He said to them: If it were beneficial, their father would beget them already circumcised from their mother. However, the true spiritual circumcision has become entirely beneficial.

Jeremiah 4:3-5 For thus saith the LORD to the men of Judah and Jerusalem, Break up your fallow ground, and sow not among thorns. Circumcise yourselves to the LORD, and take away the foreskins of your heart, ye men of Judah and inhabitants of Jerusalem: lest my fury come forth like fire, and burn that none can quench it, because of the evil of your doings. Declare ye in Judah, and publish in Jerusalem; and say, Blow ye the trumpet in the land: cry, gather together, and say, Assemble yourselves, and let us go into the defenced cities.

54. Jesus said: Blessed be the poor, for yours is the Kingdom of the Heaven.

Matthew 6:20 Then he looked up at his disciples and said: Blessed are you who are poor, for yours is the kingdom of God.

Luke 6:20 And he lifted up his eyes on his disciples, and said: Blessed are you poor, for yours is the kingdom of God.

Matthew 5:3 Blessed are the poor in spirit, for theirs is the kingdom of heaven.

55. Jesus said: Whoever does not hate his father and his mother will not be able to become my Disciple. And whoever does not hate his brothers and his sisters and does not take up his own cross in my way, will not become worthy of me.

Luke 14:26-27 If any one comes to me and does not hate his own father and mother and wife and children and brothers and sisters, yes, and even his own life, he cannot be my disciple. Whoever does not bear his own cross and come after me, cannot be my disciple.

John 17:11-21 And now I am no more in the world, but these are in the world, and I come to thee. Holy Father, keep through thine own name those whom thou hast given me, that they may be one, as we are. While I was with them in the world, I kept them in thy name: those that thou gavest me I have kept, and none of them is lost, but the son of perdition; that the scripture might be fulfilled. And now come I to thee; and these things I speak in the world, that they might have my joy fulfilled in themselves. I have given them thy word; and the world hath hated them, because they are not of the world, even as I am not of the world. I pray not that thou shouldest take them out of the world, but that thou shouldest keep them from the evil. They are not of the world, even as I am not of the world. Sanctify them through thy truth: thy word is truth. As thou hast sent me into the world, even so have I also sent them into the world. And for their sakes I sanctify myself, that they also might be sanctified through the truth. Neither pray I for these alone, but for them also which shall believe on me through their word; That they all may be one; as thou, Father, art in me, and I in thee, that they also may be one in us: that the world may believe that thou hast sent me.

56. Jesus said: Whoever has come to understand the world (system) has found a corpse, and whoever has found a corpse, is superior to the world (of him the system is not worthy).

Hebrews 11:37-40 They were stoned, they were sawn asunder, were tempted, were slain with the sword: they wandered about in sheepskins and goatskins; being destitute, afflicted, tormented; (Of whom the world was not worthy:) they wandered in deserts, and in mountains, and in dens and caves of the earth. And these all, having obtained a good report through faith, received not the promise: God having provided some better thing for us, that they without us should not be made perfect.

57. Jesus said: The Kingdom of the Father is like a person who has good seed. His enemy came by night and sowed a weed among the good seed. The man did not permit them to pull up the weed, he said to them: perhaps you will intend to pull up the weed and you pull up the wheat along with it. But, on the day of harvest the weeds will be very visible and then they will pull them and burn them.

Matthew 13:24-30 He put before them another parable: The kingdom of heaven may be compared to someone who sowed good seed in his field; but while everybody was asleep, an enemy came and sowed weeds among the wheat, and then went away. So when the plants came up and bore grain, then the weeds appeared as well. And the slaves of the householder came and said to him, Master, did you not sow good seed in your field? Where, then, did these weeds come from? He answered, An enemy has done this. The slaves said to him, Then do you want us to go and gather them? But he replied, No; for in gathering the weeds you would uproot the wheat along with them. Let both of them grow together until the harvest; and at harvest time I will tell the reapers, Collect the weeds first and bind them in bundles to be burned, but gather the wheat into my barn.

58. Jesus said: Blessed is the person who has suffered, for he

has found life. (Blessed is he who has suffered to find life and found life).

Matthew 11:28 Come to me, all you that are weary and are carrying heavy burdens, and I will give you rest.

59. Jesus said: Look to the Living-One while you are alive, otherwise, you might die and seek to see him and will be unable to find him.

John 7:34 You will search for me, but you will not find me; and where I am, you cannot come.

John 13:33 Little children, I am with you only a little longer. You will look for me; and as I said to the Jews so now I say to you, Where I am going, you cannot come.

60. They saw a Samaritan carrying a lamb, on his way to Judea. Jesus said to them: Why does he take the lamb with him? They said to him: So that he may kill it and eat it. He said to them: While it is alive he will not eat it, but only after he kills it and it becomes a corpse. They said: How could he do otherwise? He said to them: Look for a place of rest for yourselves, otherwise, you might become corpses and be eaten.

61. Jesus said: Two will rest on a bed and one will die and the other will live. Salome said: Who are you, man? As if sent by someone, you laid upon my bed and you ate from my table. Jesus said to her: I-Am he who is from that which is whole (the undivided). I have been given the things of my Father. Salome said: I'm your Disciple. Jesus said to her: Thus, I say that whenever someone is one (undivided)
he will be filled with light, yet whenever he is divided (chooses) he will be filled with darkness.

Luke 17:34 I tell you, on that night there will be two in one bed; one will be taken and the other left.

62. Jesus said: I tell my mysteries to those who are worthy of my mysteries. Do not let your right hand know what your left hand is doing.

Mark 4:11 And he said to them, To you has been given the secret of the kingdom of God, but for those outside, everything comes in parables.

Matthew 6:3 But when you give alms, do not let your left hand know what your right hand is doing.

Luke 8:10 He said, To you it has been given to know the secrets of the kingdom of God; but for others they are in parables, so that seeing they may not see, and hearing they may not understand.

Matthew 13:10-11 Then the disciples came and said to him, Why do you speak to them in parables? And he answered them, To you it has been given to know the secrets of the kingdom of heaven, but to them it has not been given.

63. Jesus said: There was a wealthy person who had much money, and he said: I will use my money so that I may sow and reap and replant, to fill my storehouses with grain so that I lack nothing. This was his intention (is what he thought in his heart) but that same night he died. Whoever has ears, let him hear!

Luke 12:21 Then he told them a parable: The land of a rich man produced abundantly. And he thought to himself, What should I do, for I have no place to store my crops? Then he said, I will do this: I will pull down my barns and build larger ones, and there I will store all my grain and my goods. And I will say to my soul, Soul, you have ample goods laid up for many years; relax, eat, drink, be merry. But God said to him, You fool! This very night your life is being demanded of you. And the things you have prepared, whose will they be? So it is with those who store up treasures for themselves but are not rich toward God.

64. Jesus said: A person had houseguests, and when he had prepared the banquet in their honor he sent his servant to invite the guests. He went to the first, he said to him: My master invites you. He replied: I have to do business with some merchants. They are coming to see me this evening. I will go to place my orders with them. I ask to be excused from the banquet. He went to another, he said to him: My master has invited you. He replied to him: I have just bought a house and they require me for a day. I will have no spare time. He came to another, he said to him: My master invites you. He replied to him: My friend is getting married and I must arrange a banquet for him. I will not be able to come. I ask to be excused from the banquet. He went to another, he said to him: My master invites you. He replied to him: I have bought a farm. I go to receive the rent. I will not be able to come. I ask to be excused. The servant returned, he said to his master: Those whom you have invited to the banquet have excused themselves. The master said to his servant: Go out to the roads, bring those whom you find so that they may feast. And he said: Businessmen and merchants will not enter the places of my Father.

Luke 14:16-24 Then Jesus said to him:, Someone gave a great dinner and invited many. At the time for the dinner he sent his slave to say to those who had been invited, Come; for everything is ready now. But they all alike began to make excuses. The first said to him, I have bought a piece of land, and I must go out and see it; please accept my regrets. Another said, I have bought five yoke of oxen, and I am going to try them out; please accept my regrets. Another said, I have just been married, and therefore I cannot come. So the slave returned and reported this to his master. Then the owner of the house became angry and said to his slave, Go out at once into the streets and lanes of the town and bring in the poor, the crippled, the blind, and the lame. And the slave said, Sir, what you ordered has been done, and there is still room. Then the master said to the slave, Go out into the roads and lanes, and compel people to come in, so that my house may be filled. For I tell you, none of those who were invited will taste my dinner.

Matthew 19:23 Then Jesus said to his disciples, Truly I tell you, it will be hard for a rich person to enter the kingdom of heaven.

Matthew 22:1-14 And Jesus answered and spake unto them again by parables, and said, The kingdom of heaven is like unto a certain king, which made a marriage for his son, and sent his servants to call those who were invited to the marriage feast; but they would not come. Again he sent other servants, saying, Tell those who are invited, Behold, I have made ready my dinner, my oxen and my fat calves are killed, and everything is ready; come to the marriage feast. But they made light of it and went off, one to his farm, another to his business, while the rest seized his servants, treated them shamefully, and killed them. The king was angry, and he sent his troops and destroyed those murderers and burned their city. Then he said to his servants, The wedding is ready, but those invited were not worthy. Go therefore to the thoroughfares, and invite to the marriage feast as many as you find. And those servants went out into the streets and gathered all whom they found, both bad and good; so the wedding hall was filled with guests. But when the king came in to look at the guests, he saw there a man who had no wedding garment; and he said to him, Friend, how did you get in here without a wedding garment? And he was speechless. Then the king said to the attendants, Bind him hand and foot, and cast him into the outer darkness; there men will weep and gnash their teeth. For many are called, but few are chosen.

65. He said: A kind person who owned a vineyard leased it to tenants so that they would work it and he would receive the fruit from them. He sent his servant so that the tenants would give to him the fruit of the vineyard. They seized his servant and beat him nearly to death. The servant went, he told his master what had happened. His master said: Perhaps they did not recognize him. So, he sent another servant. The tenants beat him also. Then the owner sent his son. He said:

Perhaps they will respect my son. Since the tenants knew that he was the heir to the vineyard, they seized him and killed him. Whoever has ears, let him hear!

Matthew 21:33-39 Listen to another parable. There was a landowner who planted a vineyard, put a fence around it, dug a wine press in it, and built a watchtower. Then he leased it to tenants and went to another country. When the harvest time had come, he sent his slaves to the tenants to collect his produce. But the tenants seized his slaves and beat one, killed another, and stoned another. Again he sent other slaves, more than the first; and they treated them in the same way. Finally he sent his son to them, saying, They will respect my son. But when the tenants saw the son, they said to themselves, This is the heir; come, let us kill him and get his inheritance. So they seized him, threw him out of the vineyard, and killed him.

Mark 12:1-9 And he began to speak to them in parables. A man planted a vineyard, and set a hedge around it, and dug a pit for the wine press, and built a tower, and let it out to tenants, and went into another country. When the time came, he sent a servant to the tenants, to get from them some of the fruit of the vineyard. And they took him and beat him, and sent him away empty-handed. Again he sent to them another servant, and they wounded him in the head, and treated him shamefully. And he sent another, and him they killed; and so with many others, some they beat and some they killed. He had still one other, a beloved son; finally he sent him to them, saying, They will respect my son. But those tenants said to one another, This is the heir; come, let us kill him, and the inheritance will be ours. And they took him and killed him, and cast him out of the vineyard. What will the owner of the vineyard do? He will come and destroy the tenants, and give the vineyard to others.

Luke 20:9-16 And he began to tell the people this parable: A man planted a vineyard, and let it out to tenants, and went into another country for a long while. When the time came, he sent a servant to the tenants, that they should give him some of the fruit of the vineyard; but the tenants beat him, and sent him away empty-handed. And he sent another servant; him also they beat and treated shamefully, and sent him away empty-handed. And he sent yet a third; this one they wounded and cast out. Then the owner of the vineyard said, What shall I do? I will send my beloved son; it may be they will respect him. But when the tenants saw him, they said to themselves, This is the heir; let us kill him, that the inheritance may be ours. And they cast him out of the vineyard and killed him. What then will the owner of the vineyard do to them? He will come and destroy those tenants, and give the vineyard to others. When they heard this, they said, God forbid!

66. Jesus said: Show me the stone which the builders have rejected. It is that one that is the cornerstone (keystone).

131

Matthew 21:42 Jesus said to them, Have you never read in the scriptures: The very stone which the builders rejected has become the head of the corner; this was the Lord's doing, and it is marvelous in our eyes?

Mark 12:10-11 Have you not read this scripture: The very stone which the builders rejected has become the head of the corner; this was the Lord's doing, and it is marvelous in our eyes?

Luke 20:17 But he looked at them and said, What then does this text mean: The stone that the builders rejected has become the cornerstone?

67. Jesus said: Those who know everything but themselves, lack everything. (whoever knows the all and still feels a personal lacking, he is completely deficient).

Jeremiah 17:5- 10 Thus saith the LORD; Cursed be the man that trusteth in man, and maketh flesh his arm, and whose heart departeth from the LORD. For he shall be like the heath in the desert, and shall not see when good cometh; but shall inhabit the parched places in the wilderness, in a salt land and not inhabited. Blessed is the man that trusteth in the LORD, and whose hope the LORD is. For he shall be as a tree planted by the waters, and that spreadeth out her roots by the river, and shall not see when heat cometh, but her leaf shall be green; and shall not be careful in the year of drought, neither shall cease from yielding fruit. The heart is deceitful above all things, and desperately wicked: who can know it? I the LORD search the heart, I try the reins, even to give every man according to his ways, and according to the fruit of his doings.

68. Jesus said: Blessed are you when you are hated and persecuted, but they themselves will find no reason why you have been persecuted.

Matthew 5:11 Blessed are you when people revile you and persecute you and utter all kinds of evil against you falsely on my account.

Luke 6:22 Blessed are you when men hate you, and when they exclude you and revile you, and cast out your name as evil, on account of the Son of man!

69. Jesus said: Blessed are those who have been persecuted in their heart; these are they who have come to know the Father in truth. Jesus said: Blessed are the hungry, for the stomach of him who desires to be filled will be filled.

Matthew 5:8 Blessed are the pure in heart, for they will see God.

Luke 6:21 Blessed are you who are hungry now, for you will be filled.

70. Jesus said: If you bring forth what is within you, it will save you. If you do not have it within you to bring forth, that which you lack will destroy you.

71. Jesus said: I will destroy this house, and no one will be able to build it again.

Mark 14:58 We heard him say, I will destroy this temple that is made with hands, and in three days I will build another, not made with hands.

72. A person said to him: Tell my brothers to divide the possessions of my father with me. He said to him: Oh man, who made me a divider? He turned to his Disciples, he said to them: I'm not a divider, am I?

Luke 12:13-15 Someone in the crowd said to him, Teacher, tell my brother to divide the family inheritance with me. But he said to him, Friend, who set me to be a judge or arbitrator over you? And he said to them, Take care! Be on your guard against all kinds of greed; for one's life does not consist in the abundance of possessions.

73. Jesus said: The harvest is indeed plentiful, but the workers are few. Ask the Lord to send workers for the harvest.

Matthew 9:37-38 Then he said to his disciples, The harvest is plentiful, but the laborers are few; therefore ask the Lord of the harvest to send out laborers into his harvest.

74. He said: Lord, there are many around the well, yet there is nothing in the well. How is it that many are around the well and no one goes into it?

75. Jesus said: There are many standing at the door, but only those who are alone are the ones who will enter into the Bridal Chamber.

Matthew 25:1-8 Then shall the kingdom of heaven be likened unto ten virgins, which took their lamps, and went forth to meet the bridegroom. And five of them were wise, and five were foolish. They that were foolish took their lamps, and took no oil with them: But the wise took oil in their vessels with their lamps. While the bridegroom tarried, they all slumbered and slept. And at midnight there was a cry made, Behold, the bridegroom cometh; go ye out to meet him. Then all those virgins arose, and trimmed their lamps. And the foolish said unto the wise, Give us of your oil; for our lamps are gone out.

76. Jesus said: The Kingdom of the Father is like a rich merchant who found a pearl. The merchant was prudent. He sold his fortune and bought the one pearl for himself. You also, seek for his treasure which does not fail, which endures where no moth can come near to eat it nor worm to devour it.

Matthew 13:45-46 Again, the kingdom of heaven is like a merchant in search of fine pearls; on finding one pearl of great value, he went and sold all that he had and bought it.

Matthew 6:19-20 Do not store up for yourselves treasures on earth, where moth and rust consume and where thieves break in and steal; but store up for yourselves treasures in heaven, where neither moth nor rust consumes and where thieves do not break in and steal.

77. Jesus said: I-Am the Light who is over all things, I-Am the All. From me all came forth and to me all return (The All came from me and the All has come to me). Split wood, there am I. Lift up the stone and there you will find me.

Author's Note:

Many scholars believe the order of verses 30 and 77 were misplaced and these two verses should be connected as one verse.

30. Jesus said: Where there are three gods, they are gods (Where there are three gods they are without god). Where there is only one, I say that I am with him. Lift the stone and there you will find me, Split the wood and there am I.

137

John 8:12 Again Jesus spoke to them, saying, I am the light of the world. Whoever follows me will never walk in darkness but will have the light of life.

John 1:3 All things came into being through him, and without him not one thing came into being.

78. Jesus said: Why did you come out to the wilderness; to see a reed shaken by the wind? And to see a person dressed in fine (soft – plush) garments like your rulers and your dignitaries? They are clothed in plush garments, and they are not able to recognize (understand) the truth.

Matthew 11:7-9 As they went away, Jesus began to speak to the crowds about John: What did you go out into the wilderness to look at? A reed shaken by the wind? What then did you go out to see? Someone dressed in soft robes? Look, those who wear soft robes are in royal palaces. What then did you go out to see? A prophet? Yes, I tell you, and more than a prophet.

79. A woman from the multitude said to him: Blessed is the womb which bore you, and the breasts which nursed you! He said to her: Blessed are those who have heard the word (meaning) of the Father and have truly kept it. For there will be days when you will say: Blessed be the womb which has

not conceived and the breasts which have not nursed.

Luke 11:27-28 While he was saying this, a woman in the crowd raised her voice and said to him, Blessed is the womb that bore you and the breasts that nursed you! But he said, Blessed rather are those who hear the word of God and obey it!

Luke 23:29 For the days are surely coming when they will say, Blessed are the barren, and the wombs that never bore, and the breasts that never nursed.

80. Jesus said: Whoever has come to understand (recognize) the world (world system) has found the body (corpse), and whoever has found the body (corpse), of him the world (world system) is not worthy.

Hebrews 11:37-40 They were stoned, they were sawn asunder, were tempted, were slain with the sword: they wandered about in sheepskins and goatskins; being destitute, afflicted, tormented; (Of whom the world was not worthy:) they wandered in deserts, and in mountains, and in dens and caves of the earth. And these all, having obtained a good report through faith, received not the promise: God having provided some better thing for us, that they without us should not be made perfect.

81. Jesus said: Whoever has become rich should reign, and let whoever has power renounce it.

82. Jesus said: Whoever is close to me is close to the fire, and whoever is far from me is far from the Kingdom.

John 14:6-9 Jesus saith unto him, I am the way, the truth, and the life: no man cometh unto the Father, but by me. If ye had known me, ye should have known my Father also: and from henceforth ye know him, and have seen him. Philip saith unto him, Lord, show us the Father, and it sufficeth us. Jesus saith unto him, Have I been so long time with you, and yet hast thou not known me, Philip? he that hath seen me hath seen the Father;

83. Jesus said: Images are visible to man but the light which is within them is hidden. The light of the father will be revealed, but he (his image) is hidden in the light.

84. Jesus said: When you see your reflection, you rejoice. Yet when you perceive your images which have come into being before you, which neither die nor can be seen, how much will you have to bear?

85. Jesus said: Adam came into existence from a great power and a great wealth, and yet he was not worthy of you. For if he had been worthy, he would not have tasted death.

86. Jesus said: The foxes have their dens and the birds have their nests, yet the Son of Man has no place to lay his head for rest.

Matthew 8:20 And Jesus said to him, Foxes have holes, and birds of the air have nests; but the Son of Man has nowhere to lay his head.

87. Jesus said: Wretched is the body which depends upon another body, and wretched is the soul which depends on these two (upon their being together).

88. Jesus said: The angels and the prophets will come to you, and what they will give you belongs to you. And you will give them what you have, and say among yourselves: When will they come to take (receive) what belongs to them?

89. Jesus said: Why do you wash the outside of your cup? Do you not understand (mind) that He who creates the inside is also He who creates the outside?

Luke 11:39-40 Then the Lord said to him, Now you Pharisees clean the outside of the cup and of the dish, but inside you are full of greed and wickedness. You fools! Did not the one who made the outside make the inside also?

90. Jesus said: Come unto me, for my yoke is comfortable (natural) and my lordship is gentle— and you will find rest for yourselves.

Matthew 11:28-30 Come to me, all you that are weary and are carrying heavy burdens, and I will give you rest. Take my yoke upon you, and learn from me; for I am gentle and humble in heart, and you will find rest for your souls. For my yoke is easy, and my burden is light.

Acts 15:5-17 But there rose up certain of the sect of the Pharisees which believed, saying, that it was needful to circumcise them, and to command them to keep the law of Moses. And the apostles and elders came together for to consider of this matter. And when there had been much disputing, Peter rose up, and said unto them, Men and brethren, ye know how that a good while ago God made choice among us, that the Gentiles by my mouth should hear the word of the gospel, and believe. And God, which knoweth the hearts, bare them witness, giving them the Holy Ghost, even as he did unto us. And put no difference between us and them, purifying their hearts by faith. Now therefore why tempt ye God, to put a yoke upon the neck of the disciples, which neither our fathers nor we were able to bear? But we believe that through the grace of the LORD Jesus Christ we shall be saved, even as they. Then all the multitude kept silence, and gave audience to Barnabas and Paul, declaring what miracles and wonders God had wrought among the Gentiles by them. And after they had held their peace, James answered, saying, Men and brethren, hearken unto me: Simeon hath declared how God at the first did visit the Gentiles, to take out of them a people for his name. And to this agree the words of the prophets; as it is written, After this I will return, and will build again the tabernacle of David, which is fallen down; and I will build again the ruins thereof, and I will set it up: That the residue of men might seek after the Lord, and all the Gentiles, upon whom my name is called, saith the Lord, who doeth all these things.

91. They said to him: Tell us who you are, so that we may believe in you. He said to them: You examine the face of the sky and of the earth, yet you do not recognize Him who is here with you, and you do not know how to seek in (to inquire of Him at) this moment (you do not know how to take advantage of this opportunity).

John 9:36 He answered, And who is he, sir? Tell me, so that I may believe in him.

143

Luke 12:54-56 He also said to the crowds, When you see a cloud rising in the west, you immediately say, It is going to rain; and so it happens. And when you see the south wind blowing, you say, There will be scorching heat; and it happens. You hypocrites! You know how to interpret the appearance of earth and sky, but why do you not know how to interpret the present time?

92. Jesus said: Seek and you will find. But in the past I did not answer the questions you asked. Now I wish to tell them to you, but you do not ask about (no longer seek) them.

Matthew 7:7 Ask, and it will be given you; search, and you will find; knock, and the door will be opened for you.

93. Jesus said: Do not give what is sacred to the dogs, lest they throw it on the dung heap. Do not cast the pearls to the swine, lest they cause it to become dung (mud).

Matthew 7:6 Do not give what is holy to dogs; and do not throw your pearls before swine, or they will trample them under foot and turn and maul you.

94. Jesus said: Whoever seeks will find. And whoever knocks, it will be opened to him.

Matthew 7:8 For everyone who asks receives, and everyone who searches finds, and for everyone who knocks, the door will be opened.

95. Jesus said: If you have money, do not lend at interest, but rather give it to those from whom you will not be repaid.

Luke 6:34-35 If you lend to those from whom you hope to receive, what credit is that to you? Even sinners lend to sinners, to receive as much again. But love your enemies, do good, and lend, expecting nothing in return. Your reward will be great, and you will be children of the Most High; for he is kind to the ungrateful and the wicked.

96. Jesus said: The Kingdom of the Father is like a woman who has taken a little yeast and hidden it in dough. She produced large loaves of it. Whoever has ears, let him hear!

Matthew 13:33 He told them another parable: The kingdom of heaven is like yeast that a woman took and mixed in with three measures of flour until all of it was leavened.

97. Jesus said: The Kingdom of the Father is like a woman who was carrying a jar full of grain. While she was walking on a road far from home, the handle of the jar broke and the grain poured out behind her onto the road. She did not know it. She had noticed no problem. When she arrived in her house, she set the jar down and found it empty.

98. Jesus said: The Kingdom of the Father is like someone who wished to slay a prominent person. While still in his own house he drew his sword and throughst it into the wall in order to test whether his hand would be strong enough. Then he slew the prominent person.

99. His Disciples said to him: Your brethren and your mother are standing outside. He said to them: Those here who do my Father's desires are my Brethren and my Mother. It is they who will enter the Kingdom of my Father.

Matthew 12:46-50 While he was still speaking to the crowds, his mother and his brothers were standing outside, wanting to speak to him. Someone told him, Look, your mother and your brothers are standing outside, wanting to speak to you. But to the one who had told him this, Jesus replied, Who is my mother, and who are my brothers? And pointing to his disciples, he said, Here are my mother and my brothers! For whoever does the will of my Father in heaven is my brother and sister and mother.

100. They showed Jesus a gold coin, and said to him: The agents of Caesar extort taxes from us. He said to them: Give the things of Caesar to Caesar, give the things of God to God, and give to me what is mine.

Mark 12:14-17 Is it lawful to pay taxes to the emperor, or not? Should we pay them, or should we not? But knowing their hypocrisy, he said to them, Why are you putting me to the test? Bring me a denarius and let me see it. And they brought one. Then he said to them, Whose head is this, and whose title? They answered, The emperor's. Jesus said to them, Give to the emperor the things that are the emperor's, and to God the things that are God's. And they were utterly amazed at him.

101. Jesus said: Whoever does not hate his father and his mother, as I do, will not be able to become my Disciple. And whoever does not love his father and his mother, as I do, will not be able to become my disciple. For my mother bore me, yet my true Mother gave me the life.

Matthew 10:37 Whoever loves father or mother more than me is not worthy of me; and whoever loves son or daughter more than me is not worthy of me.

102. Jesus said: Damn these Pharisees. They are like a dog sleeping in the feed trough of oxen. For neither does he eat, nor does he allow the oxen to eat.

Matthew 2:13 But woe unto you, scribes and Pharisees, hypocrites! because you shut the kingdom of heaven against men; for you neither enter yourselves, nor allow those who would enter to go in.

103. Jesus said: Blessed (happy) is the person who knows at what place of the house the bandits may break in, so that he can rise and collect his things and prepare himself before they enter.

Matthew 24:43 But understand this: if the owner of the house had known in what part of the night the thief was coming, he would have stayed awake and would not have let his house be broken into.

104. They said to him: Come, let us pray today and let us fast. Jesus said: What sin have I committed? How have I been overcome (undone)? When the Bridegroom comes forth from the bridal chamber, then let them fast and let them pray.

105. Jesus said: Whoever acknowledges (comes to know) father and mother, will be called the son of a whore.

106. Jesus said: When you make the two one, you will become Sons of Man (children of Adam), and when you say to the mountain: Move! It will move.

Mark 11:23 Truly I tell you, if you say to this mountain, Be taken up and thrown into the sea, and if you do not doubt in your heart, but believe that what you say will come to pass, it will be done for you.

107. Jesus said: The Kingdom is like a shepherd who has a hundred sheep. The largest one of them went astray. He left the ninety-nine and sought for the one until he found it. Having searched until he was weary, he said to that sheep: I desire you more than the ninety-nine.

Matthew 18:12-13 What do you think? If a shepherd has a hundred sheep, and one of them has gone astray, does he not leave the ninety-nine on the mountains and go in search of the one that went astray? And if he finds it, truly I tell you, he rejoices over it more than over the ninety-nine that never went astray.

108. Jesus said: Whoever drinks from my mouth will become like me. I will become him, and the secrets will be revealed to him.

109. Jesus said: The Kingdom is like a person who had a treasure hidden in his field and knew nothing of it. After he died, he bequeathed it to his son. The son accepted the field knowing nothing of the treasure. He sold it. Then the person who bought it came and plowed it. He found the treasure. He began to lend money at interest to whomever he wished.

Matthew 13:44 The kingdom of heaven is like treasure hidden in a field, which someone found and hid; then in his joy he goes and sells all that he has and buys that field.

110. Jesus said: Whoever has found the world (system) and becomes wealthy (enriched by it), let him renounce the world (system).

Mark 10:21-23 Then Jesus beholding him loved him, and said unto him, One thing thou lackest: go thy way, sell whatsoever thou hast, and give to the poor, and thou shalt have treasure in heaven: and come, take up the cross, and follow me. And he was sad at that saying, and went away grieved: for he had great possessions. And Jesus looked round about, and saith unto his disciples, How hardly shall they that have riches enter into the kingdom of God!

111. Jesus said: Heaven and earth will roll up (collapse and disappear) before you, but he who lives within the Living-One will neither see nor fear death. For, Jesus said: Whoever finds himself, of him the world is not worthy.

112. Jesus said: Damned is the flesh which depends upon the soul. Damned is the soul which depends upon the flesh.

113. His Disciples said to him: When will the Kingdom come? Jesus said: It will not come by expectation (because you watch or wait for it). They will not say: Look here! or: Look there! But the Kingdom of the Father is spread upon the earth, and people do not realize it.

Luke 17:20 And when he was demanded of by the Pharisees, when the kingdom of God should come, he answered them and said, The kingdom of God cometh not with observation: Neither shall they say, Lo-Here! Lo-There! For, behold, the kingdom of God is within you.

(Saying 114 was written later and was added to the original text.)

114. Simon Peter said to them: Send Mary away from us, for women are not worthy of this life. Jesus said: See, I will draw her into me so that I make her male, in order that she herself will become a living spirit like you males. For every female who becomes male will enter the Kingdom of the Heaven.

Bibliography

The Scholars' Translation of the Gospel of Thomas
by Stephen Patterson and Marvin Meyer

The Complete Gospels: Annotated Scholars Version.*
Copyright 1992, 1994 by Polebridge Press

The Other Gospels: Non-Canonical Texts. Philadelphia:
Westminster, 1982.

The New Testament and Other Early Christian Writings: A
Reader. New York: Oxford University Press, 1998.

The Apocryphal New Testament. Oxford: Clarendon, 1993.

The Gospel of Thomas: The Hidden Sayings of Jesus. San
Fransisco: HarperCollins, 1992.

 Vol. 1 of New Testament Apocrypha. Westminster/John Knox,
1991.

Nag Hammadi Library In English. San Fransisco:
HarperCollins, 1988.

Nag Hammadi Codex II,2-7 Together With XIII,2*, BRIT. LIB.
OR. 4926(1), and P.OXY. 1, 654, 655. Vol. 1. New York: Brill,
1989.

The Greek Fragments.Nag Hammadi Codex II,2-7
Edited by Bentley Layton. Vol. 1. New York: Brill, 1989.
Critical Greek Text.

The Oxyrhynchus Logoi of Jesus and the Coptic Gospel According to Thomas. London: Geoffrey Chapman, 1971.

The Sayings of Jesus From Oxyrhynchus. Cambridge: Cambridge University Press, 1920.

New Sayings of Jesus. The Oxyrhynchus Papyri. London: Egypt Exploration Fund, 1904.

The Gospel of Philip : Jesus, Mary Magdalene, and the Gnosis of Sacred Union by Jean-Yves Leloup, Jacob Needleman, Inner Traditions (August 16, 2004)

The Gospel of Philip: Annotated & Explained by Andrew Philip Smith. Skylight Paths Publishing (August 30, 2005)

Lost Scriptures : Books that Did Not Make It into the New Testament by Bart D. Ehrman. Oxford University Press, USA (October 2, 2003)

The Gnostic Gospels By Elaine Pagels. Vintage Books January 1981

The Gnostic Gospels of Jesus. By Marvin Meyer. Harper San Francisco 2005

Lost Christianities : The Battles for Scripture and the Faiths We Never Knew by Bart D. Ehrman. Oxford University Press, USA; New Ed edition (September 15, 2005)

The Gnostic Bible: Gnostic Texts of Mystical Wisdom form the Ancient and Medieval Worlds (Hardcover) by Willis Barnstone (Editor), Marvin Meyer (Editor). Shambhala; 1st edition (December 2, 2003)

The Gospel of Mary Magdalene by Jean-Yves Leloup, Jacob Needleman. Inner Traditions, March 30, 2002

The Gospel of Mary of Magdala: Jesus and the First Woman Apostle by Karen L. King. Polebridge Press November 2003

Various other sources.

ABOUT THE AUTHOR

Joseph Lumpkin has written for various newspapers and is the author of a number of books on the subjects of religion and philosophy including the best selling book, The Lost Book Of Enoch: A Comprehensive Transliteration, published by Fifth Estate Publishers.

Joseph holds his Doctorate in the field of Ministry. He lives a very full life near Birmingham, Alabama with his wife, Lynn, and his son, Breandan.

Look for other fine books by Joseph Lumpkin.

The Lost Book Of Enoch: A Comprehensive Transliteration,
ISBN: 0974633666

The Gospel of Thomas: A Contemporary Translation
ISBN: 0976823349

Fallen Angels, The Watchers, and the Origins of Evil:
A Problem of Choice
ISBN: 1933580100

Dark Night of the Soul - A Journey to the Heart of God
ISBN: 0974633631

The Tao Te Ching: A Contemporary Translation
ISBN: 0976823314

Christian Counseling – Healing the Tribes of Man
ISBN: 1933589970

Printed in the United States
50538LVS00001B/7-8

9 781933 580135